the philippine cookbook

the philippine cookbook

Second Edition

by

virginia roces de guzman
nina daza puyat

Bookmark

Second edition 2000

Introductions and side notes by Nina Daza Puyat
Book design and illustrations by May M. Tobias
Cover artwork by Katti Sta. Ana

ISBN 971-569-357-1 (pbk.)
ISBN 971-569-371-7 (sp.)

Published by The Bookmark, Inc.
264-A Pablo Ocampo Sr. Ave.
Makati City, Philippines
☎ 8958061–65
Fax: (632) 897-08-24
E-mail: bookmark@info.com.ph
Website: www.bookmark.com.ph

Printed in the Philippines by AEC Graphics

National Library of the Philippines CIP Data

Recommended entry:

De Guzman, Virginia R
      The Philippine cookbook / by Virginia Roces de
Guzman, Nina Daza Puyat. – 2nd ed. – Makati City :
Bookmark, c2000.
      1 v

      1. Cookery, Philippine. I. Puyat, Nina D. II. Title.

TX724.5.P5   641.59599   2000   P001000023
ISBN 971-569-357-1 (pbk.)
ISBN 971-569-371-7 (sp.)

05 06 07 9 8 7 6 5 4 3 2 1
0505

preface

Filipino society is basically matriarchal. The oldest woman in a clan—the matriarch—is loved, honored and, almost unhesitatingly obeyed. She holds sway over most affairs of the clan. At family get-togethers, she invariably takes center stage. On Sundays, when many clans get together for a meal, she indulges all by preparing their favorite dishes—those timeless recipes handed down by mothers to their sons and daughters.

This book is a compilation of such recipes.

Family and dear friends have generously shared a wealth of culinary gems which have little variations featured here, those extra touches and twists, that make this book different.

Collecting this wealth of material was not easy. Many recipes were described verbally. Some of the older ones made use of measures and proportions that are no longer known. We had to test each recipe to make sure that the original flavors were preserved, even after proportions were adjusted and procedures simplified to suit today's cook.

In spite of everything, we thoroughly enjoyed researching and writing this book. We know that many of you will enjoy using it, over and over, for years to come.

The Authors

contents

meats & poultry

pp. 11–52

soups

pp. 1–10

vegetables

pp. 53–67

soups

July 16, 1954
San Antonio, Texas

soups

Filipinos usually start a meal with a hot bowl of soup.
After the first serving, the soup bowl is often refilled and set down
within slurping distance. When the soup served contains pieces
of meat, fish and vegetables, the soup tureen usually remains
on the dinner table all throughout the meal, sharing equal billing
with the other courses served.

Filipinos enjoy drowning their rice in soup, or washing down spoonfuls
of food with gulps of hot broth. In a tropical country such as
the Philippines, hot soups can be a blessing for they help us perspire
and cool down. Most Filipinos wince at the thought of cold soups.
Generally we like our soup served piping hot, its enticing aroma
whetting our appetites in anticipation of a fine meal.

pancit molo

Tessie Locsin

For soup stock:
1 large chicken (preferably native)
1 large onion, quartered
1 bay leaf
1 teaspoon black peppercorns
salt

For Molo filling:

½ kilo ground pork	salt
½ kilo shrimp, peeled and minced	pepper
	soy sauce
1 head garlic, minced	2 eggs
1 large onion, minced	100 pieces Molo *wrappers*
2 stalks green onion, minced	

½ head garlic, minced	green onion, chopped
1 large onion, minced	patis

1. In a large pot, put together soup stock ingredients with water. Simmer till chicken is tender. Remove and shred. Discard bay leaf.

2. In a bowl, combine *molo* filling ingredients except wrappers. Mix very well and wrap in the *molo* wrappers. Drop in boiling soup stock.

3. In a pan, sauté garlic, onion and shredded chicken. Add to soup stock. Season with *patis* and garnish with chopped green onion. Serve with *biscocho*.

10 portions

lang-lang

Marina Reyes Antonio

1 small chicken
2 stalks celery
1 bunch spring onion
½ teaspoon peppercorns
½ kilo ground pork
⅓ kilo shrimp, shelled and chopped
2 eggs, beaten
200 grams sotanghon, soaked in water
10 grams taingang daga (wood ear mushroom),
    soaked in water
1 cup chicharo
patis
1 head garlic, sliced thinly and fried till golden brown
spring onion, chopped

1. In a casserole, put together chicken, celery, ½ bunch spring onion and peppercorns. Add about 12 cups water and bring to a boil. Lower heat and simmer till chicken is tender. Remove chicken and flake.

2. Combine ground pork, shrimp, eggs, salt and pepper. Form into small balls about ½ inch. Set aside.

3. Bring the chicken stock to a boil. Drop the pork and shrimp balls. Lower the heat and add the *sotanghon*, *taingang daga* and flaked chicken. Season with *patis*, add the *chicharo* last and do not overcook. Serve with the toasted garlic and spring onion on the side.

10 portions

crispy chicharo

Chicharo or sweet pea pods, when not overcooked, are almost as crispy as pork skin chicharon. Two sizes of Chicharo or sitsaro are available in city markets, where they are sold at comparatively more expensive prices than other greens. This delicious vegetable, grown in the cool climate of Baguio is the star ingredient in Chop Suey, *a mixed vegetable dish available in local Chinese restaurants.*

c h i c h a r o

picadillo

Pacita de Asis

$^{1}/_{2}$ kilo punta y pecho *(beef brisket)*, *cut into* $^{1}/_{2}$ *inch*
    cubes
$^{3}/_{4}$ kilo *very ripe tomatoes, chopped*
5 medium potatoes, *cut into* $^{1}/_{2}$ *inch cubes*
6 small cloves garlic, *crushed*
2 medium onions, *chopped*
salt

1. In a casserole, sauté garlic, onions and tomatoes. Cook until tomatoes are very soft. Add the meat and about 8 cups water. Simmer until meat is almost tender. Add cubed potatoes. Continue cooking till potatoes are done. Season with salt.

6 portions

dikdikan

The dikdikan, pandikdik, or almirez (mortar and pestle) is an indispensable fixture in every Filipino kitchen. Usually made of stone or marble, it is used for pounding cloves of garlic to loosen the skin, grinding peanuts for kare-kare, *pulverizing whole black peppercorns and mashing shrimp heads to obtain shrimp extract for flavoring.*

wawa's red beans

Ester Araneta

1 pack (500 grams) red beans, soaked overnight
1 whole head garlic, pierced all over with a toothpick
½ kilo pork ribs, cubed
1 piece chorizo Bilbao
1 cup olive oil
¼ cup brown sugar
½ cup vinegar
salt
pepper

1. Put beans in a large casserole with enough water to cover. Add garlic and bring to a boil. Add pork and *chorizo* and simmer till tender, 3–4 hours till beans are tender. Add more water if necessary.

2. When beans are tender, add brown sugar, vinegar and olive oil. Season with salt and pepper.

10 portions

Beans, beans

They're good for

your heart

The more you eat

The more you …

The more you …

The better you feel

So let's have beans

with every meal.

– Anonymous

caldo gallego

Pilar Araneta

$^1/_2$ kilo beef kenchi (boneless shank), cut in cubes
1 meaty ham bone
1 pack white beans (225 grams)
$^1/_2$ chicken, cut in serving pieces
1 piece chorizo Bilbao, sliced
5 medium potatoes, diced
2 radishes, diced (optional)
1 $^1/_2$ cups cooked garbanzos
$^1/_4$ kilo cabbage, shredded
1 cup olive oil

1. Soak the beans in water overnight.

2. In a large casserole, put in meat, hambone and beans. Add water to cover by about 2 inches. Bring to a boil, lower heat and simmer. When meat is almost tender, add the chicken. If the soup seems to be too thick, hot water may be added.

3. When the chicken is nearly done, add the *chorizo*, potatoes, radish, *garbanzos* and cabbage. Continue cooking until the potatoes are tender. Add the olive oil or serve on the side.

10–12 portions

chorizo bilbao

Many have the misconception that chorizo Bilbao *originated in* Bilbao, Spain. *Surprisingly, the popular* chorizo *is non-existent in that area or in other parts of Spain. Perhaps this type of sausage was what the early Spaniards imported for their cooking and then later produced commercially for local consumption. For the Filipinos,* chorizo Bilbao *refers to any dried Spanish-style pork sausage packed in paprika-tinged lard. It is used in Spanish dishes, authentic, or Filipinized, such as* paella, puchero, cocido, *etc...*

pamplina

Aquiles Dias de Rivera

1 ¹/₂ *kilos beef* pata
¹/₄ *kilo salt pork*
¹/₄ *cup olive oil*
4 *large onions, chopped*
1 *head garlic, crushed*
3 *pieces* chorizo Bilbao, *sliced*
4 *pieces potato, cubed*
1 *cabbage, cut into strips*
1 *bay leaf*
1 *pack (225 gms) white beans, soaked overnight*

1. Clean beef *pata* and put in a pot with the bay leaf. Simmer till tender, about 4 hours. Remove skin and tendons from bones and cube. Set aside the broth.

2. Boil salt pork and cube.

3. Put beans in a pot, with water to cover. Simmer till tender, about 2 hours.

4. Heat olive oil in a casserole. Sauté garlic, onions, *chorizo* and potatoes. Add broth from the *pata*.

5. Add *pata*, salt pork, cabbage. Simmer till the soup thickens. Season with salt and pepper.

12 portions

Apollo's declaration of love for Daphne: the greek goddess who was transformed into a laurel tree.

"Since you cannot be my wife
You shall assuredly be my tree
I will wear you for my crown
I will decorate you with
my harp and my quiver
And when the great Roman
conquerors lead up
The triumphal pomp to the
Capitol
You shall be woven into wreaths
for their brows
And as eternal youth is mine
you also shall be always green
and your leaf know no decay."

In Filipino cookery, the laurel or bay leaf is an essential ingredient used in adobo. *It is used for perfuming the cavity of roasted chicken and fowl and for flavoring soups and stews as part of the bouquet garni or spice bag. To extract the flavor, pump the dried leaf between moist palms or crumble into pieces before using.*

sin patria

Carmen Garcia Caro

1 kilo beef kenchi (boneless shank)
4 strips bacon
1 piece chorizo Bilbao
1 small bunch green onion
1 teaspoon peppercorns
10 cups water
$^1/_2$ cup olive oil
2 heads garlic, crushed
4 medium potatoes, cubed
2 cups cooked garbanzos
12 pieces crushed soda crackers
$^1/_4$ cup butter

1. In a pot, put kenchi, bacon, chorizo, green onion, peppercorns. Cover with water and simmer till tender, about 3 hours.

2. Remove kenchi from the pot and cube $^1/_2$ by $^1/_2$ inch. Save the broth.

3. In another pot, heat olive oil and sauté garlic till golden. Add cubed meat, broth and cubed potato. Simmer till potatoes are tender. Add garbanzos. Season with salt and pepper. Add crushed soda crackers to thicken. Add butter to enrich soup if desired.

8 portions

virgin is best

Olive oil is pressed from ripe, green olives whose trees only bear fruit after 35 years (that's why olive oil is so expensive). When buying olive oil, you must have a good eye to look for color and clarity, and also a good nose to judge the aroma.

"Extra virgin olive oil" is colored yellowish green. This means that the oil was obtained from the very first pressing of mature olives. Its flavor and aroma is intense and this precious oil must be used sparingly. "Pure olive oil" or "olive oil" is extracted from already pressed olives giving a less concentrated flavor and aroma.

sinigang na baboy

Lourdes Garcia Guevara

½ kilo cubed pork
½ kilo pork ribs
1 small bunch spring onion
1 kilo ripe tomatoes
4 pieces gabi, cut in half
½ kilo sampaloc
10 cups rice washing or water
1 bunch kangkong
1 bunch sitaw
2 pieces eggplant, cut in 1-inch pieces
2 pieces radish, cut in 1-inch pieces
patis to taste
3 pieces long green chili

1. In a large pot, put together the cubed pork, the ribs, green onion and tomatoes mashed with a fork. Cover and simmer for 30 minutes till meat is tender.

2. In another pot, put in the *sampaloc* with the water. Boil for about 10 minutes until the *sampaloc* is soft and mushy. Strain *sampaloc* water.

3. When the meat is just tender but not overcooked, pour the *sampaloc* water into the large pot. Add the vegetables according to firmness, beginning with the *gabi*, then the radish, *sitaw* and *kangkong* in the last few minutes of cooking. Season with *patis*. The chilies may be added if a hot fiery *sinigang* is desired.

10 portions

to obtain rice washing

Pour enough water into a pot of uncooked rice (bigas). Swish rice and water around with the fingers until the mixture becomes cloudy and tiny particles such as unhusked rice (palay) and tiny stones float on top. Throw out the first rinse. Repeat procedure for the second rinse but strain and save the water. This hugas bigas contains water soluble nutrients from the rice grains which give a light, somewhat viscous broth to dishes such as sinigang, dinengdeng, etc...

chicken binakol

Ado Escudero

4 cloves garlic, chopped
1/2 thumb-sized ginger, crushed
1/4 cup cooking oil
1 medium onion, sliced
1 stalk tanglad, cut into 3-inch pieces
1 chicken, cut in serving pieces
patis
pepper
6 cups rice washing
2 cups grated buko
2 cups buko water
dahon ng sili (sili leaves)
1 tablespoon spring onion, chopped

1. Sauté garlic and ginger in hot oil until brown. Add onion and *tanglad*. Add chicken, *patis* and pepper. Sauté for a while, pour rice washing, cover and simmer till chicken is tender.

2. Remove chicken and debone. Return chicken to the stock. Add *buko*, *buko* water and *dahon ng sili*. Simmer a few minutes more. Sprinkle with the spring onion before serving.

6 portions

tanglad

Tanglad or lemon grass is a plant with tall, slender leaves and a creamy, bulbous base. The lower part of the stalk is peeled and mashed to impart a lemony-earthy fragrance and flavor to soups and roasts.

sunday chicken

Nenita Matute

1 ¹/₂ kilos chicken, deboned leaving wings and legs

Stuffing:
¹/₂ kilo lean ground pork
¹/₄ kilo Chinese ham, minced
1 cup water chestnuts, chopped coarsely
¹/₂ cup onion, chopped
¹/₄ cup green onion, chopped
1 teaspoon freshly ground black pepper
1 teaspoon salt
2 egg yolks
1 Chinese pechay
1 small cabbage, quartered
2 pieces carrots, peeled
4 medium potatoes, peeled

1. Have the chicken deboned in the market. Rinse thoroughly and dry with paper towels.

2. In a bowl, combine stuffing ingredients and mix well. Pack into the chicken loosely and sew up opening.

3. In a pot, put in the chicken bones with two quartered onions and simmer about 45 minutes. Strain and discard bones. Return the stock to the pot and carefully put in the chicken. Simmer over low heat for 25 minutes. Add potatoes and carrots and when half cooked, put in the cabbage and *pechay*. Season with salt and pepper.

4. Remove the chicken from the pot and cool. Slice into half inch slices, arrange attractively on a platter with the cooked vegetables. Serve the soup in a separate tureen. The left over chicken makes great sandwiches.

10 portions

apulid

Apulid or waterchestnuts come from plants that grow on wet or swampy soil. The brown bulbs must be peeled one by one to reveal the crunchy white pith. Apulid are the size of chestnuts with the texture and flavor of turnips (singkamas).

meats & poultry

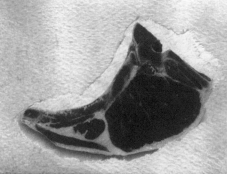

meats and poultry

In the Philippines, only pork, chicken and beef are
commercially available in almost all areas. As such, meat and
poultry dishes generally use one of these ingredients. In the provinces,
goat, deer, carabao and some other more exotic meats are
also used as alternates.

The by-products of pork, chicken and beef are also utilized
in our cooking. When an animal is slaughtered, almost
nothing is thrown away. Our frugal ways have resulted in
delicious dishes that make use of the tongue, blood,
intestines, liver, lungs, tail and other offal.

Most Filipino meat dishes are made to complement plain,
white rice. The ulam or viand must be tasty so that even
a small amount is enough to flavor a spoonful of
rice. To go a long way, meats are usually highly
seasoned and often saucy. Meats that are fried or grilled
over charcoal (inihaw) are invariably eaten with an
assortment of dipping sauces.

chicharon

Jaime V. Ongpin

1 kilo pork liempo
1 bay leaf
1 onion, quartered
4 cloves garlic

1. In a casserole, put together all ingredients. Add enough water to cover. Bring to a boil and simmer till tender, about an hour.

2. Remove the pork and drain. Leave in an airy place to dry. Slice into thin strips then $^1/_2$ inch crosswise. Refrigerate overnight.

3. Deep fat fry till golden brown. Serve with native vinegar with a few chopped *siling labuyo*.

sili

*Maliit man daw
ang sili,
Ay may anghang
na sarili.*

– Salawikain

siling labuyo

siling mahaba

siling bilog

papillote

Carmen Roces

½ kilo pork chops (5 – 6 pieces)
2 large onions, grated
2 tablespoons parsley, minced
2 hard-boiled eggs, minced
salt
freshly ground pepper
greaseproof baking paper or brown paper

1. Season pork chops with salt and pepper, set aside.

2. Fold paper, cut to the size of the pork chop with a 2-inch border all around.

3. Mix onions, parsley and egg. Coat pork chop evenly with this mixture and put on one side of the paper. Fold the other side over. Crimp and fold the edges to seal them like an *empanada*. Repeat till all the chops are wrapped. Place in a baking pan and bake at 350°F for 1½ hours. Serve the pork chops wrapped in paper.

5 portions

"Everything in a pig is good. What ingratitude has permitted his name to become a term of opprobrium?"

– de la Reyniere,
a famous epicure

caldereta de pollo

Pilar Caraballo Marquez

1 big chicken, cut into serving pieces

For marinade:
¾ cup native vinegar
4 cloves garlic
1 teaspoon freshly ground pepper
1 teaspoon salt

½ cup olive oil
4 cloves garlic
2 medium onions, chopped
½ cup tomato sauce
¼ cup liver spread
1 small can red pimientos, sliced
½ cup olives
salt
pepper

1. Combine chicken and marinade and stand 2 hours or overnight.

2. Drain chicken pieces and fry in olive oil. Set aside. In the remaining oil, sauté the garlic and onions. Add tomato sauce and liver spread. Simmer for about 15 minutes, return chicken and cook till tender. Add red pimientos and olives. Season with salt and pepper.

6 portions

some good reasons why you should learn how to cook

· to treat your boyfriend or girlfriend to a dish cooked with love

· to impress your prospective mother-in-law

· to endear yourself to your husband or wife (if you're already married)

· to cut down on eating-out expenses

· to survive and not starve when everyone is up in Baguio including the cook

· to boost your self-confidence (it feels good to know you can create something edible)

kilawin capangpangan

During Tayag

½ kilo pork kasim (shoulder), cut into small strips
¼ kilo pork liver, cut into strips
¼ kilo pork lungs, chopped fine
1 medium onion sliced
4 cloves garlic, crushed
1 teaspoon freshly ground pepper
1 bay leaf
salt

1. Marinate pork in vinegar.

2. In a pan, sauté garlic and onion. Add pork lungs, pork, vinegar, ground pepper and bay leaf. Simmer over low fire. When pork is almost tender, add liver and salt to taste. Continue cooking till pork is tender and liquid is reduced.

8–10 portions

pulutan

Whenever a group of two or more drinkers are gathered, there is pulutan. Pulutan does not quite fall under the category of appetizers nor hors d'oeuvres, but can be more accurately described as finger food to accompany alcoholic drinks.

Finger food is something that can easily be picked up by the fingers, or, if sauced or sizzling, with a fork. Pulot means to "pick up" something.

Pulutan are also called pambara or anything solid to clog one's throat. This makes for a convenient excuse to guzzle more beer or to nurse another shot of brandy.

Filipinos find every reason to drink—to celebrate a promotion, to combat depression over a lost love, to toast one on his birthday, to drown away one's problems, or to simply unwind after a hard day's work. Whether the group of men are at a neighborhood sari-sari store or at a cocktail lounge in a five-star hotel, pulutan must always be present to complement the round of drinks.

embutido

Julia Daez

¹/₂ kilo lean pork, ground
¹/₃ cup Chinese ham, minced
1 small can Vienna sausage, chopped
¹/₂ piece or 1 small chorizo Bilbao, chopped
3 egg yolks
¹/₄ cup Edam cheese, grated
3 tablespoons raisins
3 tablespoons chopped pickles
3 tablespoons shallots, chopped
8 pieces olives, chopped coarsely
2 tablespoons tomato catsup
¹/₂ teaspoon paprika
¹/₂ teaspoon Worcestershire sauce
1 ¹/₄ teaspoons salt
¹/₂ teaspoon pepper

For soup stock:
3 cloves garlic, crushed	*1 bay leaf*
1 small onion, chopped	*1 bouillon cube*
1 teaspoon vinegar	*2-3 cups water*

1. In a large casserole, sauté garlic and onion. Add vinegar, bay leaf, bouillon cube and water, simmer for 20 minutes.

2. Combine all the ingredients together in a bowl and mix well. Form into a log and wrap in aluminum foil or a cheesecloth. Lower carefully into the simmering soup stock and cook over low fire for an hour. Remove from stock and cool before slicing.

3. To make gravy, thicken remaining stock with 2 tablespoons flour dispersed in 2 tablespoons water.

8 portions

"It is not quantity of the meat, but the cheerfulness of the guests, which makes the feast."

– Lord Clarendon

ely's 1-2-3 chicken

Eligio Teehankee

10 pieces chicken wings
¹/₂ cup ginger, cut in thin strips
1 tablespoon sugar
1 tablespoon rice wine
2 tablespoons vinegar
3 tablespoons soy sauce

1. Fry chicken wings till golden brown. Remove from pan. Sauté ginger, and add the rest of the ingredients. Cover and simmer 20 minutes till wings are tender.

4 – 5 portions

ginger

Ginger is one of the world's oldest spices. It was considered very precious by the ancient Romans that it was taxed along with alcohol and tobacco. Today, it is readily available all over the world as fresh ginger root or powdered ginger. Most Westerners use ground ginger for baking breads and cookies, while fresh ginger is used for flavoring meats and fish in Asia. Since the advent of nouvelle cuisine however, adventurous cooks all over the world have experimented with ginger and incorporated it in their menus.

Depending on the recipe, fresh ginger may be smashed with the peel, sliced into rounds, cut into strips or grated. Mature ginger root has a strong flavor which can be used to eliminate fishy or gamy tastes. Young ginger has a very subtle flavor which adds interest to the taste of a dish. Young ginger roots are pale in color with light green shoots sprouting from the nodes.

One favorite Filipino beverage is made with ginger or luya: Salabat. This delicious ginger tea is traditionally taken along with bibingka or puto bumbong on cold December morning after Simbang Gabi. It is also believed that drinking salabat regularly will improve and strengthen one's voice and vocal chords.

morcon

Soledad de Guzman

1 kilo top round or sirloin beef, sliced and flattened
1 chorizo Bilbao, sliced into strips
1 large carrot, sliced lengthwise into strips
1 red bell pepper, sliced into strips
1 whole sweet pickle, cut into strips
1 hard-boiled egg, quartered
1 pork sausage or frankfurter, cut into strips

For marinade:
$^{1}/_{4}$ cup kalamansi juice
4 cloves garlic, crushed
1 teaspoon freshly ground pepper

For sauce:
3 cloves garlic, crushed
2 medium onions, chopped
6 medium tomatoes, chopped
$^{1}/_{2}$ cup tomato sauce
1 bay leaf
2 cups beef broth
breadcrumbs
salt
pepper

1. Pound beef gently to flatten with a mallet or flat side of a cleaver. Put in a bowl or plastic bag with the marinade. Let stand for 2 hours or overnight.

marinate for taste and texture

Marinades were used in the olden days to preserve meat and retard bacterial growth in the absence of refrigeration. Today, marinades are used for flavoring and tenderizing meats.

Marinating with acid partially denatures the protein in meat as it contributes to the overall taste of a dish. Some common ingredients that contain acids are vinegar, wines, kalamansi juice, catsup, tomato sauce, etc.

2. Remove beef from the marinade and lay out in a flat surface. Arrange the ingredients on top and roll up jelly roll fashion. Tie securely with string.

3. In a large pan, heat cooking oil and brown meat on all sides. Remove excess oil, add the marinade and enough water to cover the morcon. Simmer over low fire till tender for about 2 hours. When tender, remove from broth and cool. Discard string before slicing.

4. In another pan, sauté garlic, onions and tomatoes. Add tomato sauce, bay leaf and broth. Simmer for 20 minutes. Thicken with breadcrumbs, season with salt and pepper. Pour sauce over morcon.

8 portions

The secret of good cooking is first, having a love of it . . . If you're convinced cooking is drudgery, you're never going to be any good at it . . .

— James Beard

chicken encebollado

Kathy Velayo Yulo

1 kilo chicken, cut into bite-sized pieces
1/2 cup native vinegar
1 cup water
6 cloves garlic, crushed
1 medium onion, chopped
chicken giblets, chopped
1/2 cup stuffed green olives
1/4 cup breadcrumbs
salt
pepper

1. Simmer chicken in vinegar and water for 10 minutes. Drain and reserve cooking liquid.

2. Sauté garlic and onion, add chicken and giblets. Add cooking liquid and olives. Simmer till chicken is tender. Add breadcrumbs to thicken sauce. Season with salt and pepper.

5 portions

black and white pepper

Pepper comes from the Sanskrit word pippali meaning berry. Pepper bushes grow in tropical climates producing hundreds of green berries each year. These are picked just before ripening and dried out in the sun. After 10–12 days, the berries turn into the black peppercorns that we use for our adobo, tinola and atsara.

White peppercorns come from the same berries, but are allowed to ripen on the bush until they turn red. They too are dried under the sun then soaked in running water to loosen the outer shells. Traditionally, workmen trample upon the dried berries with their bare feet until the husks are completely removed (a process now done mechanically), revealing whole white peppercorns. Ground white pepper is ideal for white or light colored sauces and dressings. It is less sharp in flavor and less pungent in aroma than black pepper.

halang-halang

Judith Escaño Daez

1 chicken, cut into serving pieces
1 tablespoon ginger, crushed
1 small green papaya, peeled and sliced into 2-inch
    slices
2 cups thin coconut milk
salt
pepper
1 cup sili *leaves*

1. In a large casserole, put together chicken and ginger.
Put in enough water just to cover chicken. Simmer over
low fire, when chicken is almost tender, add *papaya*.

2. When *papaya* is cooked, pour in the coconut milk,
add *siling labuyo*, *sili* leaves and season with salt and
pepper.

6 portions

papaya

One of the more common
fruits in the Philippines,
the papaya is available all
year round. Crunchy when
unripe, it is cooked as a
vegetable, pickled as atsara
or eaten raw with rock
salt. Ripe papayas have
refreshingly sweet and tender
meat, best when eaten chilled
with a squeeze of kalamansi.
Papayas are also made into
dried fruit preserves, juices
and jams.

The enzyme papase is found
in the papaya fruit, seeds
and leaves. This is a natural
meat tenderizer that breaks
down the protein fibers in
tough cuts of beef or pork.

galantina

Dolores Veloso Paterno

1 1/2 kilos fresh chicken
1/4 cup kalamansi juice
2 teaspoons salt
1/2 teaspoon pepper

For stuffing:
1/2 kilo lean ground pork
2 pieces Vienna sausage, chopped
1 medium onion, chopped
2 tablespoons pickles, chopped
12 pitted olives chopped
2 teaspoons soy sauce
3 eggs
salt
freshly ground pepper
2 pieces whole sweet pickles, cut in strips
1 Vienna sausage, cut in strips
2 hard-boiled eggs, cut in quarters

For soup stock:
soup pack or chicken bones
1 large onion, quartered
1/2 teaspoon peppercorn

1. In a bowl marinate the chicken in *kalamansi* juice, salt and pepper.

2. In a pot put in the chicken bones, onion and peppercorn. Simmer over low fire for about 30 minutes.

Filipino High Tea

Galantina

on lightly buttered

white bread

Petite Cashew

Macaroons

Bite-sized

Pichi-pichi

Batangas barako

or Tea

21

3. In a large bowl, combine stuffing ingredients except the whole pickles, sausage strips and eggs. Taste for seasoning by making a small patty and frying it. Divide stuffing into three. Lay out the deboned chicken and cut through the center. Spread one third of the stuffing and lay out one third of the strips and eggs, alternating them to layers, ending with the stuffing. Shape the chicken into a roll and sew up the opening. Wrap tightly in cheesecloth or aluminum foil. Gently lower into the simmering broth and cook for about 1 1/2 hours. Cool and refrigerate, remove thread before slicing.

12 portions

"It is the duty of the host to make his guests feel at home.

It is the duty of the guests to remember that they are not."

– J.S. Groenfeldt

chicken pastel

Sylvia Montilla

1 chicken, cut in serving pieces
2 tablespoons soy sauce
1 tablespoon kalamansi juice
salt
pepper
2 tablespoons butter
3 cloves garlic, crushed
2 medium onions, chopped
1 cup button mushrooms, sliced
5 pieces Vienna sausage, sliced
2 pieces chorizo Bilbao, sliced
2 cups chicken broth
2 tablespoons soy sauce
3 tablespoons sherry or vino blanco
1 bay leaf
4 medium potatoes, cut into 1-inch cubes
2 carrots, sliced into $^1/_2$-inch rounds
3 tablespoons flour
$^1/_4$ cup water

For the crust:
1$^1/_2$ cups flour
$^1/_2$ teaspoon salt
$^1/_2$ cup shortening or margarine
4 tablespoons water

1. Marinate chicken in soy sauce, *kalamansi* juice, salt and pepper for at least 15 minutes.

"To invite a person into your house is to take charge of his happiness for as long as he is under your roof."

— Brillat-Savarin

2. In a casserole, brown chicken and set aside. Remove excess oil and add butter. Sauté garlic and onions, add mushrooms and sausage. Return chicken, add *chorizo*, soy sauce, broth, sherry and bay leaf. Cover and simmer chicken for about 10 minutes, add potatoes and carrots and cook till only half done. Combine flour and water and add to thicken the sauce. Simmer for a few minutes more. Adjust seasoning. Discard bay leaf and cool.

3. For crust: In a bowl, combine flour and salt. Cut in shortening or margarine with a pastry blender or two knives until mixture resembles a corn meal. Add water a tablespoon at a time, tossing lightly with a fork. Form into a ball and chill until ready to use.

4. Arrange chicken filling in a 13 × 9 × 2-inch baking dish. Roll out crust between two pieces of waxed paper and put over the chicken. Crimp the edges with the fingers or a fork to seal the edges. Brush crust with mixture of egg yolk and melted butter. Prick all over with a fork. Bake at 400°F for 20 minutes until golden brown.

6 – 8 portions

nening's chicken

Nening Pedrosa Manahan

1 large chicken, about
    1¹/₂ kilos
1 thumb-sized piece of ginger
salt
freshly ground pepper
10 pieces Chinese black
    mushrooms or dried shitake

1 head pechay Tagalog
1 cup cream
2 tablespoons butter
chicken stock or mushroom
    water

For the stuffing:
2 tablespoons butter
2 medium onions, chopped
1 small bunch leeks,
    chopped (white parts only)

¹/₂ cup *malagkit* rice
¹/₂ cup rice
2 cups chicken stock

1. Rub chicken with ginger including the cavity. Rinse and dry. Rub with salt and freshly ground pepper.

2. Soak mushrooms in hot water, when softened remove stems and put aside. Save the mushroom water.

3. For the stuffing: Sauté onions and leeks in butter. Add the *malagkit* and rice. Pour chicken stock, bring to a boil, lower heat and simmer until rice is cooked.

4. Stuff the chicken with the rice.

5. Slice the *pechay* stems and lay them at the bottom of a deep casserole, put the chicken on top. Add the mushroom stems, cream and enough chicken stock and mushroom water to cover the chicken half way. Cover and simmer until tender. Top the chicken with the *pechay* leaves and mushroom caps. Continue cooking until vegetables are done. Season with salt and pepper.

6 portions

pechay tagalog

Tagalog Pechay *belongs to the cabbage family. It's longish, wide, dark green leaves and white petiole provide a substantial amount of vitamins and minerals. Except for the base, it is almost entirely edible. Pechay leaves may be tossed in with* Nilagang Baka *and* Puchero *or used as edible wrappers for fish. It is equally delicious when chopped and cooked as* guisado.

pato binondo

Anita Young

1 duck
2 stalks leeks
2 big onions
3 medium potatoes, peeled
3 pieces ginger, sliced
4 black mushrooms, soaked in water with stems removed
$^1/_4$ cup Worcestershire sauce
$^1/_4$ cup rice wine
$^1/_3$ cup soy sauce
2 tablespoons brown sugar

1. Rinse duck and dry. Bend leeks and insert into duck cavity. Stuff in also 1 whole onion and 1 piece ginger.

2. Put duck in a bowl and add the rest of the ingredients. Let stand 10 minutes.

3. Drain duck and save marinade. In a large casserole, heat cooking oil, about 1 cup and brown duck. Remove excess oil leaving about $^1/_4$ cup.

4. Return duck to casserole. Add marinade and 1 cup water. Simmer over low fire till tender about 2 hours, turning duck once. Toward the end of cooking turn up the heat to thicken sauce.

Note: Chicken may be successfully substituted in this recipe. Cooking time will be reduced to about 45 minutes depending on the size of the chicken.

If you want your dinner,

don't offend the cook.

– Chinese proverb

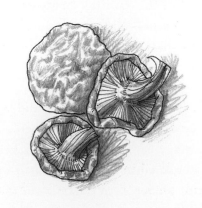

5 portions

shadylane pigeons

Jose "Chitong" Reyes

3 pigeons, cut in half
    lengthwise
$^1/_2$ cup cooking oil
1 teaspoon parsley, chopped
1 medium onion, chopped
$^1/_4$ cup celery, chopped
2 cups chicken broth

1 cup mushrooms, sliced
$^1/_4$ cup pâté de foie or
    liverwurst
2 tablespoons sherry or brandy
2 tablespoons flour
salt
freshly ground pepper

1. Heat oil and fry pigeons till golden brown. Set aside. Remove excess oil and sauté onion, parsley and celery.

2. Return pigeons to pan and add chicken broth. Simmer over low fire till tender. Add mushrooms and pâté. Thicken sauce with the flour dispersed in sherry or brandy. Season with salt and pepper.

Note: I have tried using quail for this recipe with wonderful results. You will need about 8 quails.

6 portions

Chicken stock:
$^1/_2$ kilo soup pack or chicken bones
3 medium onions, chopped
1 carrot, peeled and chopped
1 bunch parsley
1 bay leaf

1. Put all ingredients in a casserole with a cover, add 3 cups water. Simmer 30 to 45 minutes.

2. Strain stock thru a fine sieve.

parsley

pot roast

Tessie Barcelon

1 ¹/₂ kilos sirloin beef
2 tablespoons soy sauce
2 tablespoons Worcestershire sauce
1 head garlic, crushed
1 teaspoon peppercorns, crushed
¹/₃ cup flour
¹/₄ cup olive oil
4 large onions, chopped
4 cups water
1 bay leaf
¹/₄ cup white wine or sherry
2 tablespoons flour
1 cup mushrooms
2 tablespoons butter

1. In a bowl put together the meat, garlic, pepper, soy sauce and Worcestershire sauce. Marinate for about 2 hours, preferably overnight.

2. Roll meat in flour. Heat oil in a large casserole and brown meat evenly, add marinade, onions, bay leaf and water. Simmer over low fire till tender for about 3 hours. Remove meat, cool and slice.

3. Thicken sauce with the flour dispersed in wine or sherry. Season with salt and pepper.

4. To serve, arrange meat slices on a platter. Pour gravy over the meat and garnish with sautéed mushrooms.

12 portions

rellenong manok

Flor Yap

1 large chicken, (1 1/2 – 2) kilos deboned leaving only the skin

For marinade:
1/3 cup kalamansi *juice*
1 teaspoon salt

For stuffing:
1/2 kilo ground pork
1 piece chorizo Bilbao
4 pieces Vienna sausage, diced
6 hard-boiled egg yolks, mashed
1 cup galletas patatas *or soda cracker, crushed finely*
1 tablespoon grated queso de bola
1/2 cup sweet pickles, coarsely chopped
1 teaspoon freshly ground pepper
salt

For stock:
1 head garlic, crushed
2 medium onions, chopped
chicken bones

For sauce:
1 tablespoon butter
2 tablespoons flour
cooked chicken liver, mashed
1 1/2 cups chicken stock
salt
pepper

menu

SUNDAY LUNCH

Fresh Vegetable Lumpia

Sugpo sa Gata

Rellenong Manok

Buko Gulaman

1. In a bowl, marinate chicken in *kalamansi* juice and salt for an hour.

2. In a large pot, heat 2 tablespoons cooking oil and sauté garlic and onions. Add chicken bones. Pour water, about 8 cups, and allow to simmer.

3. Wrap the chicken liver in aluminum foil and cook in the stock for 20 minutes. Remove and set aside.

4. Chop *chorizo* finely and combine with the ground pork. Put in a large bowl with the rest of the stuffing ingredients. Blend very well. Make a small patty and fry to taste for seasoning.

5. Stuff chicken and sew opening, tying up the chicken as you would a parcel. Wrap in aluminum foil. Carefully lower into the simmering stock and cook for an hour.

6. When chicken is cooked, remove from stock. Allow it to cool before slicing.

7. To make the sauce, melt butter in a small casserole, add flour and stir till well blended. Gradually add stock and mashed chicken liver. Cook till thickened. Season with salt and freshly ground pepper.

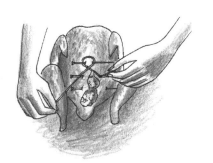

10 portions

pata with castañas

Marietta Adriano Roces

1 pork pata *from the front leg*
¹/₄ kilo lean pork, *cubed*
2 teaspoons soda

For the marinade:
¹/₂ cup soy sauce
¹/₃ cup brown sugar
1 bay leaf
1 teaspoon cracked peppercorns
250 grams castañas, *cooked and peeled*

1. Clean *pata* well and put in a bowl with the soda and enough water to cover. Let to stand for a few minutes, rinse well to remove soda and drain.

2. Return to the bowl and add the marinade. Let to stand for at least 2 hours.

3. Put pork and the marinade in a casserole. Add about 1¹/₂ cups water. Bring to a boil and then simmer till pork is tender for about 2 hours. Correct seasoning and add *castañas*.

6 portions

castañas for christmas

Castañas *or chestnuts are tender, sweet nuts covered by a fuzz-lined brittle brown shell. They are best when roasted, with the meat soft and almost chewy. In France, they are made into a delicacy called* Marrons Glacées *by glazing the cooked chestnuts in sugar.*

Castañas *are considered holiday treats in the Philippines. It has become a tradition to have chestnuts on the* Noche Buena *table along with apples and grapes, to symbolize prosperity.*

During the Japanese Occupation when importation was banned and Filipino families had very meager resources, a substitute for castañas *was invented just to keep up with the tradition of serving it during* Noche Buena. *By roasting mature coconut or* niyog *over charcoal, the flesh becomes tender and chewy, with a sweet, nutty flavor. The result:* castaniyog.

afritada

Pacita de Asis

1 kilo chicken, cut into serving pieces
$^1/_2$ kilo pork kasim (shoulder), cubed
2 large onions, quartered
1$^1/_2$ kilos very ripe tomatoes, quartered
1 whole head garlic, pricked all over with a toothpick
2 pieces bay leaf
3 tablespoons native vinegar
4 pieces potatoes, quartered
2 red peppers, cut into strips
2 green peppers, cut into strips
salt
freshly ground pepper

1. In a large casserole, brown meat. Remove, and set aside. Sauté onions and tomatoes and cook till tomatoes are very soft. Return meat. Add whole garlic, bay leaves and vinegar. Simmer till meat is half cooked. Add potatoes and cook till tender. Add red and green peppers in the last few minutes of cooking. Season with salt and pepper.

8 portions

sauté

The cooking term sauté *comes from the French word* sauter *which means "to jump." Sautéing therefore means to cook in a small amount of fat, stirring with quick movements and letting the ingredients "jump" around in the pan.*

kalderetang kambing

Annie Nakpil Tañada

2 kilos goat meat
1 cup vinegar
1 cup soy sauce
2 teaspoons freshly ground pepper
1 large head garlic
1/2 cup cooking oil
6 large onions, chopped
1 1/2 cups tomato sauce
1/2 cup tomato catsup
1/4 cup sweet pickle juice
1 cup water
2 bay leaves
1 bunch dried oregano
3/4 cup whisky
1/4 cup liver spread
2 pieces green pepper, sliced
3 pieces red pepper, sliced
1/2 cup olives
1/2 cup sweet mixed pickles
3 or 4 pieces siling labuyo
1/4 cup queso de bola, grated

1. In a nonmetallic bowl, marinate goat meat in vinegar for 15 minutes to eliminate gamy taste. Squeeze out vinegar and discard.

2. Marinate the meat in soy sauce, garlic and pepper for 45 minutes to an hour. Strain and keep marinade.

goat meat anyone?

Goat meat is popular in certain regions of the Philippines. In some areas of Metro Manila, live goats can be bought from enterprising squatter families who raise the animals on empty lots. They go for ₱900 to ₱1,500 a piece depending on the age of the goat, which should not be younger than 8 months or older than 2 years. You may have the goat slaughtered on the spot for a fee, or if you are a suki, for free.

In the provinces, the week-old baby goat or kid is castrated so that its meat will be less gamy. A day before the animal is to be butchered, it is made to drink strong Ilocano vinegar to cleanse its entrails.

Some popular Ilocano dishes make use of goat meat such as spicy kalderetang Kambing, and goat entrails such as Kilawen and Papaitan.

3. In a large casserole, heat oil and brown meat. Remove the meat and put aside. In the remaining oil, sauté onions. Return browned meat and soy marinade. Add tomato sauce, catsup, water, whisky, pickle juice *oregano* and bay leaves. Simmer till meat is tender about two hours.

4. Add liver spread, red and green peppers, olives and mixed pickles. Season with salt, pepper and minced *labuyo*. Simmer until meat is very tender but not falling off the bone. Add *queso de bola*.

10 portions

origin of oregano

Oregano *was introduced to the Filipinos by the Spaniards who came from Mexico. It is a member of the mint family and originated in the Mediterranean. The name* origanum *comes from the Greek words* orus *which means mountain, and* ganus, *which stands for joy. For the Greeks, it was truly a "joy from the mountain" where it grew lusciously wild, because they used it for cooking as well as for healing certain ailments.*

Today, oregano is used in various forms for different recipes. Whether fresh or dried, whole or ground, oregano's distinct flavor adds a special zing to any dish.

beef with eggplant

Elena Paez Tan

¼ kilo sirloin beef, sliced thin and cut in strips
5 large eggplants
1 small head garlic, minced
1 medium onion, chopped
6 medium tomatoes, chopped
2 cups beef broth or 2 cups water and 1 beef bouillon
salt
freshly ground pepper

1. Slice eggplants lengthwise and again crosswise about 1½ inches long. Put in a bowl, and sprinkle with rock salt. Let stand for a few minutes and drain. Fry eggplants in hot oil till browned, do not overcook.
Set aside.

2. In a casserole sauté garlic, onion and tomatoes. Add the beef and the broth, simmer till beef is tender. Add the fried eggplants. Season with salt and pepper.

6 portions

ALIOPHILE – garlic lover

ALIOPHOBIA – fear of garlic

There is a famous court case in the United States where a restaurant that used garlic liberally was sued by aliophobics. The aliophiles, of course, protested and rallied behind the case. Eventually, the court ruled that the odor of garlic was beneficial to civilization.

tondo-tondo

Inocencia Reyes Roces

$^{1}/_{2}$ kilo chicken thighs, deboned
$^{1}/_{4}$ kilo chicken liver
$^{1}/_{4}$ kilo chicken gizzards
$^{1}/_{2}$ kilo lean pork

For marinade:
$^{1}/_{2}$ cup soy sauce
$^{1}/_{2}$ cup kalamansi juice
2 tablespoons Worcestershire sauce
1 small head garlic, crushed
1 teaspoon freshly ground pepper

1. Cut the chicken, liver, gizzards and pork into uniform cubes about $^{3}/_{4}$ inch. Put in a bowl and add marinade. Stand a few hours or overnight.

2. Skewer alternately into short barbecue sticks 4–5 inches long. Grill over live coals or broil in the oven.

Tondo-Tondo is usually served with *sinigang*. It also makes an interesting cocktail dish.

5 portions

t.i.p.s

Leaving tips for waiters and

bellboys is the best way

To Insure Prompt Service.

binagoongan

Kathy Velayo Yulo

1 kilo pork, cubed
8 cloves garlic, crushed
$^1/_2$ cup vinegar
1 $^1/_2$ cups water

4 cloves garlic, crushed
1 small onion, chopped
2 tablespoons bagoong
1 teaspoon peppercorns

1. In a pan put together pork, garlic, vinegar and water. Simmer for 30 minutes. Drain pork and reserve broth.

2. Sauté garlic and onion. Add *bagoong* and cook for 5 minutes. Add pork, broth and peppercorns. Simmer till pork is tender.

6 portions

kanin

Bahaw man daw at

magaling,

daig ang bagong-saing.

Lamig man daw at tutong,

masarap din sa taong

gutom.

– Salawikain

2 tablespoons
bagoong

lengua estofada

Carmen Gonzalez

1 ox tongue, about 1 kilo
1/2 cup flour
1/2 cup olive oil
6 cloves garlic, crushed
2 medium onions, chopped
1 small can tomato sauce
1 tablespoon vinegar
1/2 cup white wine
1 bay leaf
2 tablespoons soy sauce
1 tablespoon brown sugar
salt
pepper
1 cup button mushrooms
1/2 cup pitted olives

1. Boil water and put in ox tongue. Leave for 5–10 minutes. Rinse and scrape off white part.

2. Roll tongue in flour and brown in olive oil. Remove. In the remaining oil, sauté garlic, onions and the rest of the ingredients except mushrooms and olives. Return tongue and simmer over low fire till tender.

3. When tongue is tender remove and slice. Thicken sauce with 2 tablespoons flour if necessary. Add the mushrooms and olives. Season with salt and pepper. Return sliced tongue.

8 portions

38

foreign tongues

In the early civilizations, people already cooked and ate tongues of animals and birds. The most highly prized delicacy during the Roman Empire were the tongues of flamingos. In 14th century France, pig tongues were very popular but were later suspected to be the culprit of the leprosy epidemic. Meat inspection then became de riguer *and* that is why even today, meat inspectors are known as langueyeurs *or literally,* tongue inspectors.

In 15th century Italy, pork tongues were served in lavish feasts while whale tongues became special fare for the French in the 16th century. In the 1800s, French gastronomes raved over carp tongue, serving it only to the most distinguished guest at a banquet. In the United States, American Indians traded buffalo tongue for whisky from the early settlers.

kebabs

Minda Vaswani

$^1/_2$ kilo ground beef or ground pork
1 medium potato, chopped fine
1$^1/_2$ teaspoons ginger, minced
3 cloves garlic, minced
$^1/_2$ teaspoon sugar
salt
pepper
2 eggs
barbecue sticks

For sauce:
1 tablespoon butter
1 cup tomato sauce
2 teaspoons kalamansi *juice*
3 pieces siling labuyo, *chopped or hot sauce*
salt

1. Combine kebab ingredients together and mix well.
Form into 3-inch logs and skewer on barbecue sticks.
Cook over live coals or broil till done.

2. Put together sauce ingredients and simmer for
15 minutes. Serve sauce on the side.

6–8 portions

non-stick barbecue grill

To prevent barbecued meats

and fish from tearing and

sticking to the grill, brush

grill generously with oil

before using.

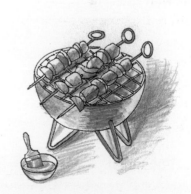

quekiam

Adelina Reyes Cruz

¼ kilo shelled shrimp
¼ kilo pork fat, minced
½ cup flour
2 eggs
2 teaspoons salt
1 teaspoon pepper
1 teaspoon sugar
atsuete *(optional)*

1. Shell shrimps and chop coarsely. Put in a bowl with the pork fat. Add flour, eggs, salt, pepper, sugar. Mix thoroughly and make a small patty and fry to check the seasoning.

2. Form small patties and fry in hot oil. Drain well and put over paper napkins to absorb the oil. Serve hot with sauce on the side.

For sauce:
1 big radish grated finely
1 cup vinegar
½ cup sugar
1 ½ teaspoon salt

1. Put grated radish in a bowl. Sprinkle with salt and let stand for 5 minutes then squeeze out juice. Put in a colander and wash out salt. Drain.

2. Return radish to bowl. Add vinegar, sugar and salt.

6 portions

sangkalan

Long before the advent of those hard plastic chopping boards, Filipinos used to use (some continue to do so, especially in the wet markets) wooden ones called sangkalan. The commercial ones were shaped and polished into perfect rectangles and rounds, with a hole at the handle for hanging. But there were those "crude" sangkalans which were slices of large tree trunks or branches mostly from sturdy trees like sampaloc, acacia, caimito. These were the cheapest, most available woods that were durable enough to withstand constant slicing and pounding and chopping.

The modern sangkalan is lighter in weight and easier to clean. Hygienically speaking, these white boards are more practical and less likely to have cracks and grooves where bacteria can grow.

longganiza de hamon

Felisa Delgado

1 1/2 kilos pork kasim *(shoulder)*
2 tablespoons rock salt
2 tablespoons brown sugar
5 tablespoons soy sauce
1/8 teaspoon salitre
1/4 cup white wine

longganiza de recado

1 1/2 kilos pork kasim *(shoulder)*
4 tablespoons *Spanish* paprika
1 1/2 tablespoons garlic, crushed
2 tablespoons salt
1/8 teaspoon salitre
1/4 cup white wine

1. Remove the tough outer skin of the pork, leaving the fatty layer. Grind the pork finely or pass thru the steel blade of a food processor.

2. In a large bowl combine the ground pork and the rest of the ingredients and mix thoroughly. Cover the bowl with aluminum foil or plastic wrap and keep in the refrigerator a few hours or overnight.

3. Cut squares of waxed paper about 6 × 4 inches. Form pork mixture into logs and roll in waxed paper. Store in the refrigerator or freezer. Each recipe makes about 48 longganizas.

A typical Filipino breakfast consists of sinangag *(garlic fried rice) using* bahaw *or leftover rice from the night before, scrambled or fried egg and a meat or fish viand with a dipping sauce of native vinegar and crushed garlic.*

The viand can be any of the following: beef tapa, pork tocino, beef or pork longganiza, daing na bangus or dried salted fish. Also considered breakfast fare are canned goods like sautéed corned beef or sautéed sardines and fried luncheon meat.

Some may opt for a lighter breakfast of pan de sal *and* kesong puti *with coffee or* ensaymada *with hot cocoa, but to the Pinoy who needs to work a long day, nothing can be more satisfying than a full meal to start the day. And a full meal to any Pinoy is incomplete or not filling enough without a healthy serving of rice.*

tapia's meat balls

Martin Tinio

¹/₄ kilo ground pork
¹/₄ kilo shrimp, shelled and chopped fine
2 medium tomatoes, seeded and chopped
1 medium onion, minced
1 small singkamas, *minced*
1 teaspoon salt
egg

For the sauce:
¹/₂ cup native vinegar
1 small onion, thinly sliced
7 teaspoons sugar
1 teaspoon salt
¹/₄ teaspoon pepper

1. Mix all ingredients together and form into ³/₄ inch balls. Deep fry in hot oil and drain in paper towels or napkins.

2. Mix all sauce ingredients together and serve on the side.

The meatballs in this recipe may be used in *misua* soup. Substitute 1 tablespoon flour for the egg and drop the meatballs in boiling broth instead of frying.

The carajay or kawali is a shallow wok made of heavier, thicker metal. It is the Filipino housewife's favorite cooking companion used in making sinangag, *sauteing vegetables, frying meats and fish and simmering saucy dishes like* afritada *and* menudo.

c a r a j a y

beef tapa

Patricia Daza

1 kilo sirloin beef, sliced thin
2 tablespoons soy sauce
2 tablespoons rock salt
1 1/2 tablespoons sugar
4 cloves garlic, crushed
1/2 teaspoon pepper

Put all ingredients in a bowl and mix well. Keep in the refrigerator for at least 2 days before frying.

acharra

1 medium green papaya, grated
1 small carrot, grated or cut into flower shapes
1 green pepper, cut into fine strips
1 small bunch shallots (sibuyas Tagalog), peeled

For pickling solution:
2 teaspoons ginger, cut into fine strips
1 cup vinegar
1/4 cup sugar
1/4 cup rock salt

1. In a bowl put all vegetables together. Sprinkle with rock salt and let stand for a few hours or overnight.

2. Squeeze out excess liquid from the vegetables and rinse in water to remove salt.

3. Put all pickling solution ingredients together. Stir till sugar and salt are dissolved. Pack vegetables in jars and pour vinegar mixture to cover. Refrigerate. Serve 2–3 days later.

TAPSILOG —

Tapa, Sinangag, Itlog

LONGSILOG —

Longganiza, Sinangag, Itlog

TOSILOG —

Tocino, Sinangag, Itlog

TAPSI-TURBI —

Tapa, Sinangag-Turon,

Bibingka

PANKAPLOG —

Pan de Sal, Kape, Itlog

menudo sulipeña

Gene Gonzales

1 kilo oxtail
2 tablespoons butter
1 head garlic, chopped
1 medium onion, chopped
1 piece red pepper, cubed
1 piece green pepper, cubed
1 cup chorizo Bilbao, diced
1 cup tomato sauce
1 cup cooked garbanzos
salt
pepper

1. Clean and wash oxtail. Pressure cook for about 20–25 minutes or simmer with enough water to cover till tender. Debone and cut into ½ inch cubes.

2. In a casserole heat butter and sauté garlic and onion, add red and green peppers. Stir fry 2–3 minutes. Add *chorizo* and oxtail and tomato sauce. Simmer over low fire for about 10 minutes, add *garbanzos*. Season with salt and pepper.

6 portions

turo-turo, point-point

Whether it be in an air-conditioned fastfood center in Makati, a roadside carinderia along Pampanga or a makeshift stall beside the Pantranco Bus Terminal in Quezon City, the principle behind the turo-turo is the same. Point-point.

An array of hot dishes is displayed before the hungry diner. All he has to do is point to the viands which appeal to him and these are dished out accordingly.

Each dish has a corresponding price, excluding the cup of rice. A bowl of soup is sometimes included.

The Pinoy turo-turo. Service is fast and personalized. The food is inexpensive but filling. Who said fast food originated in America?

adobong antigo

Martin Tinio

1 kilo chicken or pork, cut in serving pieces
¹/₄ cup vino blanco or 5-year-old rum
4 teaspoons soy sauce
5 cloves garlic, crushed
2 teaspoons salt
1 teaspoon freshly ground pepper
1 cup vinegar
1 cup buko juice
1 small head garlic, crushed

1. Marinate the meat in the *vino blanco* or rum, soy sauce, garlic, salt, pepper and vinegar, for at least 2 hours. Drain.

2. Fry meat till golden, pour off excess oil and add *buko* juice. Simmer till tender and *adobo* begins to give off oil. Fry the extra garlic and sprinkle on the *adobo* before serving.

5 portions

BEACH PICNIC

Adobong antigo

Steamed shrimps

Burong manga

Salted eggs and tomato salad

Rice wrapped in banana leaves

Ripe mangoes

roast turkey

1 turkey (12 – 16 pounds)
1 thumb-sized piece of ginger
salt
freshly ground pepper
$^1/_2$ cup melted butter

1. Rub turkey all over with the ginger, including the cavity. Rinse and pat dry. Rub with salt and freshly ground pepper. Fill cavity with stuffing, do not pack the stuffing too tightly as it expands while cooking. Sew up cavity. Brush turkey with soft butter and place in a roasting pan breast side up. Roast in a pre-heated oven (425°F) for twenty minutes reduce heat to 325°F basting every 30 minutes. Allow 20 minutes cooking time per pound. Cover the turkey with aluminum foil if it is browning too soon.

rice stuffing

Nening Pedrosa Manahan

1 kilo ground pork
2 cups celery, chopped
6 medium onions, chopped
2 cups cooked rice

3 teaspoons sage
salt
pepper

1. In a casserole cook the pork and render its fat. Add the celery and onions. When the vegetables are soft stir in the rice, season with sage, salt and pepper.

Rice obtained by crookedness will not boil up into good food.

— Chinese proverb

spanish style stuffing

Jesus Marcos Roces

3 stalks celery, chopped
2 big onions, chopped
1 head garlic, crushed
1 kilo lean ground pork
1 1/2 cups tomato sauce
1/4 kilo ham, chopped
1 cup raisins
2 tablespoons capers
1 cup button mushrooms, sliced
salt
pepper

1. Sauté celery, onions and garlic. Add the ground pork and cook until no more pink shows. Add the tomato sauce and simmer for 10-15 minutes. Add the rest of the ingredients, season with salt and pepper.

celery

Celery, raw,

Develops the jaw,

But celery, stewed,

Is more quietly chewed.

– Ogden Nash

gravy

turkey giblets
turkey liver
2 onions, chopped
2 stalks celery, chopped
$^1/_2$ teaspoon peppercorns
3 cups water
$^1/_4$ cup cornstarch
2 tablespoons brandy or rum
salt
pepper

1. In a casserole, put together the giblets, onions, celery, peppercorn and water. Bring to a boil and simmer till giblets are tender. Add the liver and continue cooking for another 20 minutes until the liver is cooked. Remove giblets and liver and chop finely, set aside. Strain the stock.

2. In a casserole, put together the pan drippings from the roast, and the stock, bring to a boil and add the cornstarch dispersed in 2 tablespoons water. Add the brandy or rum and season with salt and pepper, return the chopped giblets and liver.

menu

NEW YEAR'S DAY

LUNCH

*Wawa's Red Beans
(beans, they say, are good
luck to eat for the new year)*

Beachcomber Salad

*Roast Turkey with
Spanish stuffing*

*Twelve Grapes
signifying the months of the
year*

Natilla

huevos al plato

Teresita Morato Lazatin

2 tablespoons olive oil
4 cloves garlic, crushed
1 medium onion, chopped
1 small can tomato sauce
1 bay leaf
2 pieces chorizo Bilbao, *sliced and fried*
1 cup green peas
salt
freshly ground pepper
6 eggs

1. Sauté garlic and onion in olive oil. Add tomato sauce and bay leaf. Simmer 15 minutes. Discard bay leaf and season with salt and pepper. Add the fried *chorizos* and the peas.

2. Spread tomato sauce mixture on 9-inch pie plate or baking dish. Break the eggs carefully on top of the sauce. Bake at 350°F for 20 minutes or until eggs are firm.

The discovery of a new dish is more beneficial to humanity than the discovery of a new star.

— Anonymous

adobong moderno

Maria Margarita Pineda

1 kilo chicken thighs
¹/₂ cup native vinegar
2 tablespoons soy sauce
1 small head garlic, crushed
¹/₂ teaspoon salt
¹/₂ teaspoon ground pepper

¹/₂ cup water
1 eggwhite, beaten
¹/₂ cup flour
¹/₂ cup cornstarch
¹/₂ teaspoon salt
¹/₂ teaspoon ground
    pepper

1. In a saucepan, combine chicken, vinegar, soy sauce, garlic, salt and pepper. Bring to a boil and simmer. When mixture dries up, add water and continue cooking for about 15 minutes until chicken is tender.

2. Remove chicken from pan and strain remaining sauce. Put aside.

3. Debone chicken and cut in half. Combine flour, cornstarch, salt and pepper. Dip chicken in eggwhite and dredge in the dry ingredients. Fry in hot oil until golden and crisp.

Adobo *dip:*

1 cup mayonnaise
¹/₄ cup adobo *sauce*
2 tablespoons parsely, minced
1 teaspoon garlic, minced

1. Combine ingredients and serve with the *adobo*.

5 portions

Taken from Encyclopedia del Idioma © 1958-Aguilar, S. A., Ediciones Madrid

El caldo de vinagre, sal, pimenton, ajos, etc... que para sazonar y conservar carnes y otras cosas; la misma carne: contenia lomo en adobo.

pork tortilla

Ida Caro de Guzman

2 tablespoons olive oil or vegetable oil
¹/₄ kilo lean ground pork
4 large cloves garlic minced
2 large onions chopped fine
4 – 5 tomatoes
1 teaspoon salt
¹/₄ teaspoon freshly ground pepper
5 large eggs

1.   Heat oil and sauté garlic, do not allow to brown. Add onions and cook till soft. Add tomatoes and continue cooking until soft and mushy.

2.   Add pork and cook about 10 more minutes. Season with salt and pepper.

3.   Lightly oil a 6" non-stick pan. Beat eggs with a fork or a whisk until frothy. Stir in pork mixture. Heat up pan, pour in tortilla mixture. Cook over medium heat, lowering heat if the bottom is browning too fast.

4.   When the bottom is golden brown, flip tortilla upside down into a plate. Then quickly slide back into the pan to cook the other side. Not to worry if the tortilla breaks, it will all come together when fully cooked.

Serve hot as an entree or cool to room temperature cut into squares and serve as appetizers. Leftovers make good sandwiches, too.

There is no love sincerer than the love of food.

– George Bernard Shaw

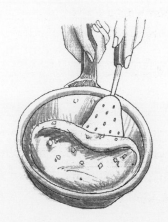

siomai

Bella Vasquez

3 pieces dried mushrooms
750 grams ground pork
500 grams fresh shrimps, peeled and chopped fine
1 medium singkamas, chopped fine
1 ¹/₂ tablespoons oyster sauce
¹/₂ teaspoon salt
¹/₂ teaspoon sugar
1 egg
2 tablespoons cornstarch
1 pack wanton wrapper
1 small carrot grated

1. Soak dried mushrooms in hot water for 15 minutes. Drain and chop fine.

2. Mix all ingredients together except wrappers and carrots. Put a heaping teaspoonful of the pork mixture in the center of the wrapper. Press lightly to form a waist. Flatten top with the back of a spoon. Garnish with a little grated carrot.

3. Arrange siomais on a cloth lined steamer. Steam for 20 minutes. Makes about 20 pieces. Serve with soy sauce and calamansi.

vegetables

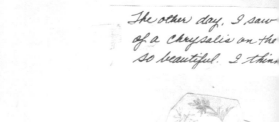

The other day, I saw
of a chrysalis on the
so beautiful. I think

that enhance the flavor
transfather found.

vegetables

Vegetables have always been a part of the Filipino diet, being inexpensive, nutritious readily available and a good source of fiber. An extensive variety of greens, fruits, and tubers are available in city markets, supermarkets and even in neighborhood sari-sari stores. In the provinces, most families grow their favorite vegetables right in their own backyards.

For everyday cooking, vegetables are usually cooked *guisado*, *guinataan* or *pinakbet*. Curiously, we are not much of salad eaters even if we have access to fresh vegetables all year long. We like our vegetable dishes cooked and served hot. To many families, a vegetable dish spiced up with pork, shrimp, fish or *bagoong*, is the main viand.

fresh vegetable lumpia

Luz Guevara

1 head garlic, crushed
1 cup shrimp, boiled
  and peeled
1/2 cup liempo (pork bely),
  boiled and cut in
  small cubes
3 tablespoons atsuete seeds
  soaked in 1/2 cup water
1 large carrot, cut in
  julienne pieces
1/4 kilo string beans, cut
  in julienne pieces

1 large singkamas, cut in
  julienne pieces
1 cup chicharo, cut in
  julienne pieces
1/4 kilo cabbage, shredded
2 medium potatoes, boiled
  and cut in cubes
2 pieces tokwa, cut in fine
  strips and fried
1 cup garbanzos, cooked
2 heads Tagalog lettuce
lumpia wrappers

For sauce:
1/2 cup brown sugar
2 tablespoons soy sauce

2 tablespoons cornstarch
2 cups water

1. In a large pan or a wok, sauté garlic, shrimps and pork. Strain *atsuete* and add *atsuete* water. Simmer for 10 minutes. Add vegetables in recipe order. Taking care not to overcook vegetables. Add salt to taste.

2. In saucepan, combine sugar, soy sauce and 1 1/2 cups water. Heat and bring to a boil. Add the cornstarch dispersed in the remaining water. Cook till thickened.

3. Put a lettuce leaf on the *lumpia* wrapper and top with the vegetable filling. Roll tucking in one end leaving the other end with the lettuce peeking. Serve with the sauce and minced fresh garlic on the side.

12 portions

Bahay kubo
kahit munti
Ang halaman doon
ay sari-sari

Singkamas at talong
Sigarilyas at mani
Sitaw, bataw, patani.

Kundol patola
Upo't kalabasa
At saka mayroon pang
Labanos mustasa.

Sibuyas kamatis
Bawang at luya
At sa paligid-ligid
Ay mayroon pang linga.

– Filipino Folk Song

ajete (salsa monja)

Aquiles Diaz de Rivera

2 pieces loaf bread, crusts removed
2–3 tablespoons vinegar
2 cloves garlic, crushed
1 teaspoon sugar
$^1/_2$ teaspoon salt
$^1/_3$ cup olive oil
freshly grated nutmeg
$^1/_2$ cup small shallots, peeled
$^3/_4$ cup vinegar
$^1/_2$ cup olives (110 grams)

1. In a non-metallic bowl, soak bread in vinegar for 3–4 hours or overnight, covered with cloth or plastic wrap.

2. Squeeze out excess vinegar from bread and discard. Mix with finely crushed garlic, sugar and salt. Add olive oil a little at a time, stirring constantly. Season with freshly grated nutmeg.

3. Boil the vinegar and add the peeled shallots. Turn off heat and leave shallots to cool in the vinegar. Drain.

4. Add shallots and olives to the bread mixture. Blend well and store in an airtight jar and refrigerate. Serve with roasts or steamed seafood.

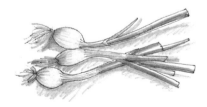

a special salsa

In 1621, Sor Geronima de la Asuncion, a monja or cloistered nun of the Sta. Clara order from Toledo, Spain, came to the Philippines to spread Catholic doctrine and in the process, culinary expertise as well. The Sta. Clara nuns set up the first monastery in Intramuros, probably the one referred to by Jose Rizal in Noli Me Tangere as the beaterio where Maria Clara was supposed to have stayed.

The monastery's music maestro, a certain Bonifacio Agustin, learned the Salsa Monja recipe from Sor Geronima. He passed this on to his children and his grandchildren. Aquilles "Achi" Dias de Rivera is Bonifacio's great grandson and he unselfishly shares with us this precious family heirloom.

pinangat

Asuncion Vera Perez

For filling:
5 gabi *leaves, chopped*
$^1/_4$ *kilo cooked shrimp, shelled*
$^1/_2$ *kilo* liempo *(pork bely), boiled and cut into strips*
bagoong
8 cloves garlic, crushed
2 medium onions, chopped
1 tablespoon ginger, cut into strips
1 teaspoon siling labuyo, *chopped*
1 $^1/_2$ cups thick coconut milk

12 – 15 gabi *leaves*
gabi *stalks*
thin coconut milk

1. In a bowl combine all the filling ingredients.

2. Choose *gabi* leaves making sure they have no holes.
Put about $1^1/_2$ tablespoons of filling in the center and fold
like a letter, overlapping the sides to make a square of
about $2^1/_2 \times 2^1/_2$ inches. Tie with strips taken from the
gabi stalks.

3. In a casserole put a layer of *gabi* stalks at the bottom.
Arrange the *gabi* packets on top. Add just enough thin
coconut milk to cover. Simmer without stirring till
cooked and coconut milk thickens.

8 portions

If you are buying from the wet market, choose those that are already wilted but not so dry that the leaves crumble. Vendors hang them from a pole on the stalls until they are ready to be sold. Medium-sized leaves are best because the stalks of the bigger ones tend to be fibrous, while the small ones are not large enough for wrapping. If you happen to have fresh leaves, dry them first under the sun for a day to eliminate the itchiness it may cause the throat upon ingestion.

lumpiang ubod

Adelina Reyes Cruz

For filling:
1/4 kilo pork fat, cut in
    small cubes
1 head garlic, crushed
1 piece tokwa, *sliced into*
    thin strips and fried
3 big alimasag, steamed
    and meat flaked
1/4 kilo shrimp

1/4 kilo chicharo, *sliced*
    into thin strips
1 kilo ubod, *sliced into*
    thin strips
patis
2 heads Tagalog *lettuce*
wansoy
lumpia *wrappers*

For sauce:
2 pieces panocha
2 cups water

1/2 cup soy sauce

1. Put cubed pork fat in a casserole and cook over medium heat to render fat. When pork fat is browned and crisp, remove from pot and drain.

2. Shell the shrimps. Put shrimp heads and shells in a mortar and pound with a little water to extract juice. Set aside.

3. Sauté in pork fat, garlic, *tokwa*, shrimp, crab. Add *chicharo*, *ubod* and shrimp juice. Cook only until vegetables are crisp tender. Season with *patis*. Remove from fire and cool.

4. Wash Tagalog lettuce and dry. Put a leaf on a *lumpia* wrapper and top with the filling add *wansoy* if you wish. Roll wrapper tucking in one end leaving the other end with the lettuce peeking.

5. In a small saucepan crumble *panocha*. Add water and soy sauce. Cook over medium heat till syrupy. Serve sauce on the side with chopped roasted peanuts and crushed garlic.

12 portions

panocha

Panocha *are the dark, solid sugar cakes that are made from the juice of sugar cane. The juice is collected and then boiled down until concentrated, leaving a thick natural sugar syrup that is poured and allowed to harden in whole or half brown coconut shells. These are used as a sweetener-flavorings for drinks such as* sago-gulaman *and for native* kakanin. *These are also mixed with peanuts and formed into round, flat, brittle candies.*

langka salad

Judith Escaño Daez

1 unripe langka, *about 5 cups, peeled and cut*
1 ¹/₂ – 2 cups thick coconut milk
1 red bell pepper, cut into strips
1 ¹/₂ tablespoons onion, chopped
2 medium tomatoes, chopped
1 ¹/₂ tablespoons vinegar
1 teaspoon salt

1. Boil *langka* in water and salt. When tender remove from fire and drain.

2. Put *langka* in a serving bowl, combine with the rest of the ingredients. Refrigerate and serve cold.

8–10 portions

enjoying jackfruit

The langka, nangka or jackfruit is perhaps one of the largest fruits in the world. It grows to about 1 ¹/₂ – 2 feet long with short spines covering its body.

When ripe, it gives off a very distinct aroma. The fruit is often wrapped with plastic while still hanging from the tree to prevent birds and insects, which cannot resist the sweet smell, from feasting on the succulent flesh. Langka is delicious cooked as preserves for halo-halo or eaten au naturel soaked in a bed of ice.

The unripe langka's whitish pulp is usually cooked as a vegetable stewed in coconut milk with shrimps and pork. The large langka seeds are boiled till tender, peeled and eaten with sugar.

laing

Daisy Olaguer

1 kilo gabi *leaves*
2 cups thin coconut milk
1 cup thick coconut milk
4 cloves garlic, crushed
2 pieces daing, *cut into 4 pieces*
3 – 4 pieces siling labuyo
salt

1. To prepare *gabi* leaves, hang out on the sun for an hour until the leaves are dry and feel brittle. Remove leaves from stalks. Cut only the tender parts of the stalk to about 2 inches long.

2. In a casserole, combine all ingredients except *gabi* leaves and stalks. Cook over a low flame stirring constantly for 10 minutes until mixture is thick and oily.

3. Add *gabi* stalks first and cook till tender. Add leaves and cook for another 10 minutes. Season with salt.

8 portions

how to obtain thin and thick coconut milk

Fresh coconut milk, essential to Filipino dishes and desserts, is obtained from mature coconut or niyog. *First, grate the* niyog *using the special coconut grater (a low stool with a rounded, toothed blade) or have it grated mechanically in the market. Add one cup of water per grated nut and mash with clean hands. Squeeze out the first extract and strain through a fine sieve or cheesecloth. This is called the* unang piga *or* kakang gata *and is usually added last to a dish for final thickening.*

Next, add two cups of water to the same grated coconut meat. Repeat the procedure and reserve the thinner coconut milk. This is commonly used for initial boiling of meats, fish, vegetables and fruits.

Iaswa

Sylvia Montilla

2 medium onions, sliced
4 tomatoes, chopped
2 cups water
$^1/_2$ cup sitaw, sliced into 2-inch pieces
6 pieces okra, sliced into 2-inch pieces
1 cup saluyot
1 eggplant, sliced into 1-inch pieces
1 cup alugbate
$^1/_2$ cup small shrimp

1. In a casserole, put together onions, tomatoes and water. Bring to a boil and simmer until vegetables are soft. Add the rest of the vegetables in order of firmness. Do not overcook. Add shrimps last and season with salt.

* Great diet food. Absolutely no fat, plenty of fiber and nutritious.

5 portions

Saluyot is a bushy plant that grows in almost any type of soil. The bright green leaves are mixed in with other vegetables or sautéed with dried fish (tinapa or daing). Saluyot is a rich source of iron, calcium and vitamins, while providing a slimy texture to any dish.

Alugbati is another slimy vegetable. This red-stemmed vine can grow even in harsh conditions. It's dark green leaves are mixed with Mongo Soup or combined with steamed alimasag and shrimps.

ampalaya salad

Julia Daez

1 *large* ampalaya

For marinade:

¹/₂ cup vinegar	¹/₂ teaspoon salt
¹/₄ cup sugar	pinch pepper

For dressing:

¹/₂ cup mayonnaise	3 hard-boiled eggs, chopped
2 tablespoons pickle relish	³/₄ cup small shrimp, cooked and shelled
2 tablespoons white onion, minced	salt pepper

1. Slice *ampalaya* in half lengthwise, with a melon baller scrape off all the white membrane. Wash and dry *ampalaya* and keep in the refrigerator overnight.

2. Slice *ampalaya* thinly. Put in a bowl and sprinkle with salt. Mash with the hand to extract juice. Wash off the salt with water and drain.

3. In a casserole, boil water and add a pinch of baking soda. Drop *ampalaya* and cook for about 5 – 7 minutes. Drain and refresh with tap water.

4. Put together marinade mixture in a bowl and add drained *ampalaya*. Marinate for 3 – 4 hours in the refrigerator.

5. Drain *ampalaya* very well. Mix in with the dressing ingredients and pile over a lettuce lined bowl. Serve well chilled.

6 portions

ampalaya: love it or leave it

"You're either going to love it or you're going to hate it." So goes the warning to those who try ampalaya *for the first time. Also known as* amargoso *or* bittermelon, *this highly nutritious vegetable has a bitter taste that is unique—totally repulsive for some, but irresistible to others.* Ampalaya *lovers claim that to acquire a taste for it, you must give it a second and third chance and it must be cooked properly to be enjoyed.*

To temper the bitter bite, soak the ampalaya *slices in warm water with salt before cooking or mash with rock salt to squeeze out the bitter juice. When buying* ampalaya, *choose those that have wrinkles that are more spread out.*

bicol express

Cely Kalaw

¹/₄ kilo long sili
¹/₂ cup pork, sliced in strips
3 cloves garlic, crushed
1 medium onion, chopped
2 cups thick coconut milk
2 teaspoons bagoong

1. Remove stems from the *sili* and cut lengthwise to remove seeds. Slice into ¹/₂-inch pieces.

2. In a casserole combine the pork, garlic, onion and coconut milk. Bring to a boil, lower the heat and simmer until pork is tender. Add the sliced *sili* and continue cooking until *sili* is soft and sauce is thickened. Add the *bagoong* to taste.

6 portions

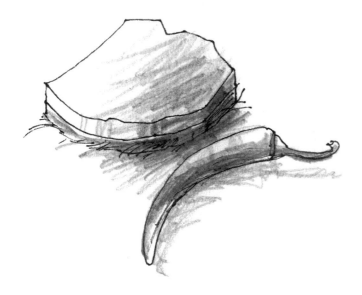

bicol express

It has been taken for granted that the dish "Bicol Express" originated in Bicol and is an indigenous recipe from that region. Cely Kalaw, owner of The Grove - Luto ng Inay, the restaurant that first served this fiery concoction, is actually from Los Baños. She and her brother Demitrio invented "Bicol Express"— a dish that would be the perfect partner for Laing.

The society matrons of Manila in the 1960s frequented the original location of The Grove in M.H. del Pilar. They complained that the Laing was delicious, but too spicy for their taste. So, brother and sister decided to adjust to their customers and cut down on the peppers of Laing. But what about those clients who want to eat hot dishes?

This prompted them to concoct a complementary dish that could be added to Laing so that the spiciness could be controlled. The more of it you add to Laing, the hotter Laing will be. The problem was solved.

"Pero, anong ngalan nito?" Cely asked her Kuya Itring. Just then, a train from nearby Paco Railway Station, choo-chooed by, whistling to them. It bore the name "Bicol Express."

star salad

Rachy Cuna

¹/₄ kilo sigarilyas
1 cup small shrimp cooked and shelled
1 bunch watercress
2 tablespoons red pepper, chopped

For dressing:
3 tablespoons vinegar
1 tablespoon soy sauce
2 tablespoons sugar
¹/₂ teaspoon ground pepper
¹/₄ cup corn oil

1. Slice *sigarilyas* crosswise into stars. Blanch and drain thoroughly.

2. In a serving bowl, arrange the *sigarilyas*, watercress and shrimps. Combine dressing ingredients and pour over salad. Sprinkle red pepper.

4–5 portions

sigarilyas

This four-cornered vegetable pod is also known as the "winged bean" or "asparagus bean." It is delicious simply sautéed with bits of pork and shrimps. When not overcooked, it has an interesting mouthfeel with its four-winged shape and desirable crunch.

sweet sour mango

1 cup sugar
1 cup water
burong mangga

1. In a pan put together sugar and water and make a light syrup. Cool.

2. Add cooled syrup to *burong mangga* and refrigerate. Store a few days before serving.

burong mangga

Very green carabao mangoes, cut in thick strips
rock salt
sterilized bottles

1. Put together green mangoes and rock salt. Let stand overnight. Next day, pack into sterilized bottles and refrigerate.

2. To sterilize bottles: Put bottles and lids in a large casserole. Add water to cover and boil for 20 minutes. If plastic lids are to be used, add 5 minutes. Cool bottles and lids.

some like it green

Like the dog's conditioned response in Pavlov's experiment on classical conditioning, many Pinoy mouths water at the mere mention of "manggang hilaw." Although we love ripe mangoes for dessert, unripe mangoes are always welcome just to munch on in between meals or to complement a meal.

Some like their mangoes green and crunchy, sour as sour can be. Others prefer them with a tinge of yellow, sour and dour with a hint of sweetness. Part of the fun of eating unripe mangoes is the "Bite-pucker-grimace-shudder" reaction.

The perfect match for manggang hilaw *is of course,* bagoong alamang *sautéed with lots of garlic and pork. It's a combination that is as inseparable as salt and pepper or strawberries and cream. However, some like to have their own* sawsawan *of rock salt,* patis, suka, sugar, *or a combination of these.*

A recent development on the green mango is its elevation into a fruit juice shake, served in first-class hotels and restaurants. Slightly tart, slightly sweet, it is a refreshing drink which can certainly do without a douse of bagoong.

panara

Salome Limgenco Tan

1 ¹/₂ kilos upo
2 medium onions, chopped
4 cloves garlic, crushed
1 cup shrimp, peeled and chopped
¹/₂ cup ground pork
salt
pepper
lumpia *wrappers*

1. Grate *upo* coarsely. Leave in a colander and allow to drain.

2. In a saucepan, sauté garlic and onions. Add pork, shrimp and *upo*. Simmer for about 10 minutes until the liquid that comes from the *upo* is reduced and mixture is dry. Remove from heat and cool.

3. Top one side of the *lumpia* wrapper with the *upo* filling. Roll tucking in both ends. Seal other side by moistening wrapper. Deep fat fry until golden. Drain on paper towels to absorb excess oil.

6 portions

In the provinces, the upo *or bottle gourd vines are allowed to climb up a trellis where the vegetable-fruit can hang from the slatted bamboo roof. Empty bottles are hung beside the fruits in the belief that the upo will try to outdo and outgrow their neighbors. Furthermore, the bottles are supposed to keep the upo company and should prevent the young fruits from falling prematurely.*

gising-gising

Pricilla Carpio Castillo

1 large bundle kangkong
¹/2 cup pork belly sliced thin and cut into strips
1 large onion chopped
1 large garlic cloves minced
1 cup coconut milk
3–4 siling mahaba *or green chili cut into matchsticks*
patis *or* bagoong

1. Using a thin sharp knife cut *kangkong* lengthwise into 4 pieces.

2. Put pork and water to cover in a saucepan. Simmer until pork is tender. Pour off water and continue cooking until pork gives off oil. Add a little cooking oil if pork is sticking to the pan. Add garlic and onions and cook until vegetables are soft. Add coconut milk, and simmer until slightly thickened. Add chilis and *kangkong* and season with *patis* or *bagoong*.

It is hard to say what it is about chilies that causes an addiction. Perhaps it is the exquisite pain they bring that heightens the pleasure of eating, but once you have enjoyed them, there is no turning back: you are hooked forever.

– Madhur Jaffrey

kangkong

green mango salad

Virginia Roces de Guzman

2 cups green mango cut into matchsticks
¼ cup hibe or dried shrimps
3 tablespoons shallots sliced fine
1 tablespoon crushed panocha or brown sugar
1 tablespoon patis
lime juice
1–2 siling labuyo *chopped*
2 tablespoons peanuts chopped
2 tablespoons toasted garlic
1 bunch wansoy or coriander

1.   Prepare dressing by putting together shallots, lime juice, panocha and *patis*. Adjust the ingredients to suit your taste.

2.   Pan fry the hibe in a little oil. Cool and set aside. Arrange the mango in a serving dish. Top with the rest of the ingredients. Pour dressing over and serve.

gulay na bayabas

Penny Velasco Laperal

1 kilo ripe guavas
1 tablespoon coarse salt or sea salt
¹/₂ kilo pork tocino
1 head garlic peeled and pounded
1 cup sugar

1. Peel guavas, cut in half and scoop out the seeds. Chop fine and mix in the salt. Set aside.

2. Slice tocino into bite-sized pieces. Put in a saucepan with enough water to cover. Bring to a boil, lower heat and simmer until tender. Pour off extra water, continue cooking until tocino gives off oil and is nicely browned.

3. Remove tocino from the pan and sauté garlic until soft. Return tocino to the pan and add the guavas. When the guavas have softened add the sugar and cook until consistency is thick like jam.

This condiment is similar to chutney and is usually served with fried bangus.

The discovery of a new dish does more for the happiness of the human race than the discovery of a star.

– Anthelme Brillat-Savarin

fish
& seafood

...well I didn't plant
...d four days of
... I h..d planted two

She only recogniz...
...all. It is the only plac...

fish and seafoods

With more than 7,000 islands in the country, it is not
surprising to find our wet markets and supermarkets teeming
with an extensive variety of fish and shellfish. Fortunately,
they can be bought fresh practically anywhere in the
country at any time of the year.

Fish is sold in various ways, usually whole with head
and tail intact. Large fish may be cut as fillets and steaks,
while heads and tails are sold separately. The *Bangus* or milkfish,
found exclusively in our waters, can be prepared by the
vendor as split, daing-style, or skinned whole for
relleno. Your favorite *suki* will gladly scale and
eviscerate your purchase.

In the Philippines, fish and seafood are cooked in
very simple ways. Since fish and seafood are always
fresh, there is no need to mask off flavors. We have always been
spoiled by this privilege. Perhaps this is the reason why we
were never challenged enough to create elaborate
dishes, believing that subtle flavor enhancers are
what bring out the best in freshness.

rellenong alimasag sa gata

Divi Guytingco

1 kilo alimasag (4 – 5 pieces)
1 onion, chopped
4 cloves garlic, chopped
¼ kilo ground pork
1 cup buko, scraped with a spoon and chopped coarsely
1 egg
salt
freshly ground pepper
1 thumb-sized piece of ginger
1 teaspoon labuyo, chopped (optional)
2 – 3 cups coconut milk

1. Steam the crabs. Carefully remove the shell and flake the meat. Do not remove the claws and the legs.

2. In a bowl, combine the crabmeat, onion, garlic, ground pork, buko, egg, salt and pepper. To test the seasoning, make a small patty and fry.

3. Return the crabmeat mixture to the shells. Tie securely with string and carefully arrange in a covered casserole. Pour the coconut milk, add the ginger and labuyo and bring to a boil. Cover and simmer the first ten minutes, then uncover and continue cooking until sauce thickens.

* Left over stuffing makes a tasty filling for cocktail-sized lumpias.

4 – 5 portions

he, she, and it crabs

To differentiate male from female crabs, look for the "apron" found on their backsides. Males have pointed "aprons" while females have a stouter, heart-shaped "aprons." Female crabs command a premium price because they contain the delicious, but cholesterol-laden aligi or crab coral. Occasionally, by a quirk of nature, you will find male crabs with this precious roe. These ones are mischievously called bakla.

sinaing na tulingan

Linda Saludo Tangco

½ kilo tulingan
   (small tuna)
2 tablespoons rock salt
50 grams pork fat,
   sliced into strips
¼ teaspoon freshly
   ground pepper

¼ cup tamarind juice
3 cloves garlic
1 medium onion, sliced
1 thumb-sized ginger, crushed
2 pieces siling mahaba
½ cup water

1. Remove gills and all internal organs of the fish. Slit both sides of the fish and press against the sides with palms of the hands to flatten the fish and soften its flesh. Wash thoroughly under running water, till water runs clear. Rub fish with salt in and out.

2. In a saucepan, arrange the pork fat at the bottom. Put the fish on top side by side. Add the rest of the ingredients. Bring to a boil, lower the heat and simmer for about 30 minutes till fish is done.

For the tamarind juice:
Boil 100 grams of sampaloc in ½ cup water and strain.

paho salad

10 pieces green paho
4 shallots, sliced thinly

3 small tomatoes, sliced
rock salt

1. Combine all ingredients and serve with the *tulingan*.

4 portions

tulingan

Tulingan *belongs to the species of the tuna family. Tulingan is a fatty fish, but when cooked, its meat is somewhat dry. Its flavor can be compared to chicken that tuna is sometimes referred to as the "chicken of the sea." The medium-sized tulingan are usually cut up into fish steaks, while the large ones are sold whole to Japanese restaurants to be cut into expensive sashimi. The fresh fish heads also make delicious* Sinigang *soup. Of course, tulingan also ends up in your pantries as canned tuna.*

adobong hito

Carmen Roces

3 medium-sized hito
1 small head garlic, crushed
¹/₄ cup yellow ginger juice
³/₄ cup native vinegar
¹/₂ cup pork lard
salt
pepper

1. In the market, have the head and gills of the fish removed. Also remove the internal organs of the fish and wash it well. Let stand in vinegar for 30 minutes, drain and rub with coarse salt till slimy coating is removed. Rinse in vinegar again then wash fish in water.

2. In a bowl marinate the fish in garlic, ginger juice and enough vinegar to cover. Let stand for an hour. Drain and reserve marinade.

3. Heat pork lard and fry fish until crisp. Remove fish from pan and put out excess lard. Pour in the marinade and bring to a boil, simmer uncovered till the vinegar evaporates. Add *hito* and continue cooking till oil is clear.

4–5 portions

catch a catfish

Locally known as hito, catfish are scaleless and slimy, mud-colored, flat-headed fish with whiskers. Although they are not much to look at, their white flesh is tasty and delicious, fried or simply broiled over charcoal.

Market vendors keep them sliding and slithering in plastic basins filled with fresh water, where the housewife can point to which unfortunate hito she would like to take home. The vendor then catches the fish, holds it steady with one hand, and with expert aim, hits the helpless, hapless catfish on the head with the flat side of her knife, causing instant death.

sinanglay

Lulu Silverio

1 carp or Tilapia 1¹/₂ – 2 kilos
4 medium onions, chopped
5 medium tomatoes, chopped
6 cloves garlic, chopped
1 head pechay Tagalog
1 tablespoon ginger, cut in strips
kamias sliced (optional)
siling labuyo (optional)
¹/₂ cup vinegar
1 cup thin coconut milk
2 cups thick coconut milk
salt
pepper

1. Scale and clean fish, rub in rock salt to remove fishy smell. Split the fish from head to tail, *daing* style. Wash well.

2. In a bowl put together onions, tomatoes and garlic. Season with salt and pepper. Stuff the fish with this mixture and wrap in the *pechay* leaves.

3. Put the fish in a large casserole and top with the ginger strips and *kamias*. Pour the vinegar and thin coconut milk over the fish and simmer till almost done. Add thick coconut milk and continue cooking till done. Season with salt and pepper.

8 portions

what to do when a fish bone gets caught in your throat

Try any of the following and find out which one works best for you:

1. Swallow a big lump of banana or a clump of cooked rice. The bone should get dislodged as the food goes down your throat.

2. Ask a breech-born person (one who came out of his mother's womb with the feet instead of the head first) to massage your throat. Old folks say that those who were born "suhi" have the special power to displace things that are stuck.

3. While at table, do not announce to those present that you have a fish bone caught in your throat. Quietly turn your plate 360 degrees and the bone will miraculously be gone.

kinilaw

Edith Fabella Pelaez

*¹/₂ kilo very fresh espada or tanguige, cut in ¹/₂-inch
    cubes*
¹/₃ cup native vinegar
¹/₃ dayap juice
dayap peel, cut in strips
1 small onion, chopped fine
2 teaspoons ginger, sliced into fine strips
salt
freshly ground pepper
siling labuyo chopped
1 cup thick coconut milk

1. Clean the fish under running water very well.
Combine all ingredients in a non-metallic bowl and chill.
Serve on a bed of lettuce as an appetizer.

If going to the fish market is too much trouble. Start
with tuna sashimi from your favorite sushi bar. You save
time and effort.

6 portions

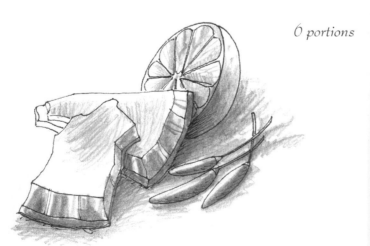

*KINILAW and KILAWIN
come from the root word
hilaw or raw. This suggests
a manner of cooking, or
rather, non-cooking of
seafood. The fish or shellfish, which must not be
anything but fresh, is
marinated in acids such as
vinegar and kalamansi juice
to "cook" the delicate flesh.
Chopped raw onions, chilli
peppers and herbs such as
fresh coriander leaves or
wansoy are sometimes
added to enhance the flavor
of the dish.*

*Pork meat and pig's entrails
are seasoned the same way
as kilawin but they must
first be boiled till tender.
Pork is never eaten raw or
medium rare because it may
be infected with parasites,
particularly the trichina
worm, which is eliminated
only upon thorough cooking.*

bagoong alamang

Inocencia Reyes Roces

1 *kilo fresh* alamang
¹/₂ cup rock salt
¹/₃ cup kalamansi *juice*
¹/₄ kilo pork fat
6 cloves garlic
¹/₃ cup kalamansi *juice*
¹/₄ cup vinegar
atsuete *(optional)*
siling labuyo *(optional)*

1. Put fresh *alamang* in a flat dish and pick out shells and bits of stone. Do not wash. Sprinkle salt and *kalamansi* juice and mix very well. Cover with plastic wrap and leave to ferment in the refrigerator for a day or two.

2. Cut pork fat into small cubes. Put in a pan and cook over medium heat to render fat. Strain oil and set aside the pork cracklings.

3. Return oil to the pan and heat. If you wish to use *atsuete*, put about a teaspoon and fry. Remove when the oil takes in the color. Sauté garlic but do not brown. Add *alamang*, *kalamansi* juice, vinegar and *siling labuyo* if you wish. Adjust the salt to taste. Pour into sterilized bottles and cool. Keep in the refrigerator.

bagoong

Amoy ng bagoong maingat

mang takpan,

pilit na sisingaw pagdating

ng araw.

rellenong bangus

Concepcion Verano

1 bangus (at least 1 kilo)
6 cloves garlic, crushed
2 medium onions, chopped
1/4 kilo ground pork
1 small carrot, chopped
1/2 cup water chestnuts, chopped
1/2 cup raisins
2 hard-boiled eggs, sliced

For the marinade:
1/4 cup kalamansi juice
2 tablespoons soy sauce

1. Have the bangus deboned in the market. Wash the skin well and put in a bowl with the marinade.

2. In a casserole, put in the bangus flesh with a teaspoon of salt and about a cup of water. Simmer till the fish is cooked. Cool. Drain the fish and flake carefully picking out the bones.

3. Sauté the garlic and onions. Add the pork, and cook till no more pink shows. Add the flaked bangus, carrots and waterchestnuts. Cook a while longer, add the olives and raisins. Season with salt and pepper.

4. Stuff bangus skin. Arrange the sliced eggs on top and sew up the opening with a needle and thread. Fry bangus till golden brown or bake at 350°F for 15–20 minutes till brown.

8 portions

menu

BALIKBAYAN *LUNCH*

Chicken Binakol

Laing

Rellenong Bangus
Served with Acharra

Kalderetang
Kambing

Maja Blanca

baked fish with clam sauce

Carmen Cuyugan von Kaufmann

1 red snapper or Apahap *about 1 kilo*
2 teaspoons rock salt
1 teaspoon freshly ground pepper
¹/₄ cup kalamansi *juice*
¹/₂ cup clam broth
4 tablespoons butter, softened
1 medium onion, chopped
1 small carrot, cut in fine strips
1 green pepper, chopped
2 cups shrimp, cooked and peeled
2 cups clams, cooked and shucked
1 cup white wine

1. Clean fish. Rub with salt, pepper, *kalamansi* juice and 2 tablespoons butter. Put in a baking dish and bake at 375°F basting once in a while with clam broth.

2. In the pan sauté the vegetables in the remaining butter. When the carrots are half cooked, add shrimps and clams. Add wine and simmer.

3. Arrange the clam and shrimp mixture on top of the fish. Cover with a buttered aluminum foil and return to the oven and bake a few minutes longer.

10 portions

Did you know that around 31 B.C. during the Roman Empire, the tablecloth was invented? The Romans loved to feast and so someone thought of covering the table with a huge bolt of cloth in order that the guests could wipe their hands and mouths after eating. Later on, guests brought their own napkins, but only to be used as wrappings to take home food.

curried crabs

Minda Vaswani

1 kilo crabs (3–4 pieces)
6 cloves garlic, crushed
2 medium onions, chopped
1 piece yellow ginger about thumb size, crushed
curry powder
3–4 pieces siling labuyo, chopped
2 cups thick coconut milk
salt

1. Clean crabs well, remove claws and cut in quarters.

2. In a large pan sauté garlic, onions, ginger and curry powder. Add *siling labuyo* and coconut milk. Bring to a boil and add crabs. Lower heat and simmer for about 20 minutes till crabs are cooked.

5 portions

Unknown to many, curry is a combination of several spices. The curry powder that is commercially available is actually a mixture of turmeric, coriander, cumin, chili, fennel and fenugreek. Other spices that are sometimes included in curry are: ginger, mustard, cloves, cardamom, allspice, mace, mustard and pepper. In India and in other Asian countries, some housewives still grind or pound whole spices to create their own secret blend.

sugpo sa gata

Regina Bernasconi Tuason

1 kilo medium-sized prawns
3 coconuts, grated
3 cups warm water
6 cloves garlic, crushed
2 medium onions, chopped
4 pieces siling labuyo, chopped
atsuete dispersed in 2 tablespoons water
salt
pepper

1. In a bowl, put grated coconut and water. Extract coconut milk and set aside.

2. In a pan, sauté garlic, onions and *siling labuyo*. Add coconut milk and simmer over low fire till mixture is thick and slightly oily and is reduced to $1/3$ its original amount. Add prawns and continue cooking till prawns are done. Season with salt and pepper.

6 – 8 portions

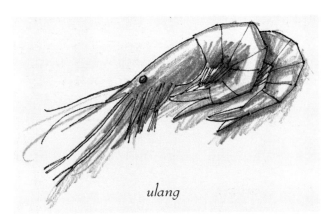

ulang

hipon

Ang hipong

natutulog,

ay tinatangay

ng agos.

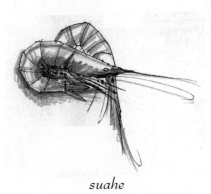

suahe

sugpo

beachcomber salad

Ditas Verzosa Chuidian

1 kilo Lapu-lapu, *filleted*
3 stalks celery with leaves
1 carrot, quartered

Dressing:
3/4 cup mayonnaise
1/4 cup olive oil
2 teaspoons mustard
1 tablespoon sugar
1/2 teaspoon salt
1/2 teaspoon white
pepper

4 medium tomatoes,
quartered
1 small bunch green onion
salt and pepper

1 tablespoon kalamansi
juice
2 tablespoons chopped
green onion
1/4 cup chopped celery
1/2 cup pineapple tidbits
2 medium apples, peeled
and cubed

The big fish

eat the little fish,

the little fish

eat the water-insects,

and the water-insects

eat the weeds and the mud.

– Chinese proverb

1. In a shallow pan put together the vegetables, salt and pepper. Add about 2 cups water and simmer for 20 minutes. Put in fish and simmer for about 15 minutes more until fish is firm and can be flaked with a fork. Be careful not to overcook. Remove from pan and cool. It will be easier to cube the fish if it chilled for a few hours.

2. In a small bowl combine mayonnaise, olive oil, mustard, salt and pepper. In a larger bowl put in cubed apples and sprinkle with *kalamansi* to prevent discoloration. Add the rest of the ingredients including fish and mayonnaise mixture. Toss lightly, and pile into a lettuce lined bowl. Serve very cold.

Note: The freshness of the fish is very important. So make an effort to go to the market to buy the best of the day's catch.

10–12 portions

bacalao a la vizcaina

Letty Lizares del Rosario

¹/₂ kilo Bacalao
1 cup olive oil
6 cloves garlic, crushed
6 medium onions, chopped
5 medium tomatoes, chopped
2 stalks celery, chopped
¹/₂ cup carrot, chopped
1 tablespoon parsley, chopped
1 teaspoon Spanish paprika
3 tablespoons tomato sauce
1 small can pimientos, sliced
¹/₂ cup almonds, sliced
1 piece biscocho, crushed coarsely

1. Soak *Bacalao* in water overnight, changing water once or twice to remove excess salt. Drain and remove bones.

2. Boil water, put in tomatoes whole. When tomatoes are softened, peel off skin, remove seeds, chop and set aside.

3. In a large casserole, heat olive oil. Sauté garlic but do not brown. Add chopped onions and lower the heat stirring frequently till onions are transparent. Add chopped tomatoes, celery, carrots, parsley and tomato sauce. Simmer over very low heat for an hour.

4. In an ovenproof dish put a layer of sauce, top with *Bacalao* and pimientos. Sprinkle almonds and *biscocho* and top with more sauce. Layer ingredients in this manner then bake at 350°F for 30 minutes.

10 portions

feast and fast with bacalao

Bacalao *is salted, dried codfish that is usually cooked with olive oil, whole tomatoes, pimientos morones (canned red peppers), garbanzos and potatoes. The imported fish has always been expensive and its a rare treat for the family to have* Bacalao. *It is usually served during Holy Week when the adults are supposed to sacrifice and abstain from eating meat. When Bacalao is part of the single meal one is allowed to have on Good Friday, then fasting becomes an easier sacrifice.*

bacalao

baked oysters

Aurora Reyes Narciso

2 tablespoons olive oil
2 medium onions, chopped
2 cloves garlic, minced
4 cups oysters, shucked
3 tablespoons butter
1 cup mushrooms, chopped
2 tablespoons flour

³/₄ cup evaporated milk
1 bunch green onions, chopped
Parmesan cheese or Edam cheese, grated
breadcrumbs

1. To clean, scrub the oysters with a brush. Put them in a large bowl and pour boiling water over them. When the shells have opened, remove the oysters, and set aside.

2. In a casserole, heat olive oil and sauté onions and garlic. Add drained oysters and cook for about 3 minutes until sides curl. Set aside. Sauté mushrooms in 1 tablespoon butter. Add to oysters.

3. In a casserole heat the remaining butter, stir in flour until well blended. Gradually add milk, stirring until mixture is smooth. Cook over low fire till thickened.

4. Combine oyster mixture and white sauce. Season with salt and pepper. Mound mixture in an oven proof dish. Sprinkle with green onions, cheese and breadcrumbs. Bake at 350°F for 15 minutes till the top is golden or broil for 5 to 10 minutes.

8 appetizer portions

love foods

The word "aphrodisiac" was derived from Aphrodite, the Greek goddess of love and beauty. It means any food or drink that arouses love and passion in a person. Nobody knows why certain foods increase sexual desires, but different cultures have different beliefs based on history and tradition.

The more common aphrodisiacs include oysters, snails and balut. Passion stimulating meats include beefy steaks, lamb, duck, goose, and organ foods such as kidney, liver, brains and tripe. The most effective love foods are those cooked with plenty of garlic, wine and those seasoned with herbs and spices.

lumpiang bangus

Carol Andrews Ferrer

1 ⅓ cups cooked
    and flaked bangus
½ cup green onions,
    chopped
2 medium tomatoes,
    chopped

1 medium onion,
    chopped
1 ½ cups sotanghon *noodles*
    cut up and softened in water
patis
pepper
lumpia *wrappers*

sauce:

½ cup sugar
½ cup water
¼ cup vinegar
½ teaspoon salt

1 clove garlic, chopped
1 – 2 pieces siling labuyo,
    chopped
¼ cup grated carrots

1. In a saucepan, put *bangus* and enough water to cover. Simmer till fish is cooked. Remove from pan and cool. Flake fish and pick out bones.

2. In another pan, heat 2 tablespoons cooking oil. Sauté garlic onions and tomatoes. When vegetables are soft, add *bangus*. Season with *patis* and pepper.

3. Drain *sotanghon* and add to *bangus*. Cook till noodles are transparent. Add green onions.

4. Cool the filling and wrap in *lumpia* wrappers. Fry in hot oil till golden brown.

For sauce:

1. In a small saucepan, combine sugar and water. Cook over medium heat until syrupy.

2. Remove from heat and add the remaining ingredients.

8 portions

Mestizang
Bangus
Madaling
Maubos

– Filipino Saying

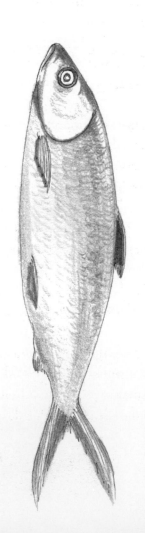

adobong pusit

Marietta Adriano Roces

1 1/2 kilos medium-sized squid
1 1/2 teaspoons baking soda
1 cup vinegar
1/2 kilo ripe tomatoes, chopped
3/4 cup olive oil
1 head garlic, crushed
2 medium onions, chopped
1/2 cup vinegar
salt
freshly ground pepper
4 pieces long green chili

1. Clean squid and separate ink. Cut into 1/2-inch rings. Put in a bowl with enough water to cover and add soda. Let stand 15 minutes. Wash out soda by rinsing in water and drain.

2. Boil vinegar and drop squid. Simmer for about 10 minutes. Strain and discard vinegar.

3. Sauté chopped tomatoes in 1/4 cup olive oil. Simmer for 20 minutes in a covered pan.

4. In a large casserole heat 1/2 cup olive oil and sauté the garlic and the onions. Add the squid, the cooked tomatoes, squid ink and vinegar. Simmer for about 20 minutes. Season with salt and pepper. Add the chilies.

10–12 portions

how to clean squid before cooking

Pull out the head from the torso. At the base of the tentacles, pick out a small ball, which is the squid's mouth or teeth. Carefully cut off the stomach hanging from under the ink sac, located directly under the head. Squeeze out the ink from the ink sac and save. Pull out the plastic membrane from the torso and discard. Wash the insides under running water. For large squids, scrape off the dark skin on the torso with a knife.

spicy 'tuyo' in olive oil

Marietta Adriano Roces

½ kilo tuyo
½ cup corn oil
½ cup olive oil
2 heads garlic, crushed
1 tablespoon labuyo, *chopped*
½ cup vinegar
1 teaspoon paprika

1.   Remove head, tail and soft parts of the *tuyo*. Fry in a little cooking oil and remove scales. Arrange in a large bottle or covered dish.

2.   In a casserole, heat corn oil and olive oil. Fry garlic until golden, add *labuyo* and vinegar. Bring to a boil and add paprika. Pour over *tuyo*, cool and store in the refrigerator. Serve after a few days to allow flavors to blend.

3.   When ready to serve, heat over low fire and sprinkle with toasted garlic.

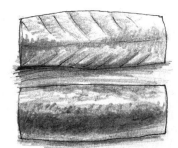

remove head, tail & soft parts of the tuyo.

---

menu

Power Breakfast

Spicy Tuyo *in olive oil*

Grilled Longganisa

Scrambled Eggs

Chunky chopped
tomatoes with native vinegar
and Siling Labuyo

Sinangag

Coffee

Si Pedro Penduko
Kumain ng tuyo
At nang hindi naligo
Iniwan ng kalaro.

— *Filipino Nursery Rhyme*

pesang isda with miso sauce

Maricor Chuapoco de los Reyes

3 cups hugas bigas *or rice washing*
1 thumb-sized piece of ginger
1 small bunch spring onions
¼ teaspoon whole peppercorns
1 kilo firm white fish (Dalag, Talakitok, Lapulapu)
1 small cabbage quartered
1 Baguio pechay
patis *or salt to taste*

1. Place rice washing, ginger, spring onions and peppercorns in a saucepan large enough to fit all the other ingredients. Bring to a boil, simmer about 10 minutes.

2. Lower fish into the broth. Add the cabbage and pechay. Cook over low heat making sure the fish is not overcooked. Season with *patis* or salt.

Miso Sauce:
1 ½ tablespoons olive oil
4 – 5 cloves garlic minced
1 large onion chopped
2 cups fresh tomatoes chopped
2 tablespoons miso or fermented soy beans
salt and pepper

1. Heat olive oil. Sauté garlic and onion until soft. Add tomatoes. Cover saucepan and allow to simmer until tomatoes are stewed. A little water may be added, if sauce is drying up. Stir in the miso, season with salt and pepper.

rice
& noodles

rice and noodles

Rice to Filipinos is a staple. It is an indispensable companion
to all viands. We don't cook with rice. Rather, we eat with rice.
We like our rice plain, boiled and white.

Most of our Filipino delicacies and desserts are
rice-based, but the few rice dishes we cook are not indigenous
to our cuisine. They are the Spanish Paella and Arroz Valenciana, or,
the Chinese Congee, Arroz Caldo or *lugao*. Rice dishes
with meat are considered complete meals.

When it comes to noodles, we are more adventurous.
From the Chinese, we developed a liking for oodles of noodles.
Our term for noodles is *pancit* and there is a *pancit canton, bihon,
sotanghon, mami, miki, Malabon, palabok* and the list goes on. They
vary in flavor, color and thickness and are made from egg, rice,
wheat or mung bean. Cooking methods vary from sautéed,
fried, steeped in a broth or topped with a sauce.
They are tossed in with meat, seafood, vegetables
or a combination of these. Filipinos love noodles because
they're delicious, filling, economical and also
fun to eat.

arroz con coliflor

Matilde Pun

For the soup stock:

Beef or pork bones or a
  combination
1 carrot, cut in 1-inch pieces

2 stalks celery, chopped
1 large onion, quartered
$^1/_2$ teaspoon peppercorns

$^1/_4$ cup olive oil
1 head garlic, crushed
2 medium onions, chopped
2 cups California rice
4 – 5 cups soup stock
$^1/_2$ kilo cauliflower divided
  into florets

$^1/_2$ cup garbanzos, cooked
1 – 2 teaspoons curry powder
1 envelope saffron
salt
pepper
2 hard-boiled eggs, sliced

1. In a casserole, put all soup stock ingredients together
and add enough water (at least 6 cups) to cover. Simmer
over low fire for 2 hours. Strain broth.

2. In a *paellera* or a large skillet, heat olive oil, sauté
garlic, and onions, add rice and cook until it becomes
opaque. Add the soup stock. Arrange the cauliflower and
garbanzos on top, sprinkle the curry powder and saffron
and season with salt and pepper. Sliced *chorizo Bilbao*
may be added if you wish. Cook the rice for about 20
minutes. Garnish with the sliced eggs.

cauliflower

5 – 6 portions

*DID YOU KNOW
THAT in the olden days,
there were no individual
plates for guests? In ban-
quets, everyone ate from
common platters of food that
were passed around.*

*In the fifteenth century, a
special kind of thick, hard
bread was given out to
guests who used them as a
plate for their food. At the
end of the feast, these
breads soaked with
drippings from the meats
would be given away to
beggars who would hang
around the kitchen door.*

spaghetti edgardo

Dr. Edgardo Fores

¹/₂ cup butter
1 cup button mushrooms, sliced
1 cup black olives, sliced
4 pieces chorizo Bilbao, sliced
1 ¹/₂ cups tomato sauce
1 cup heavy cream
salt
freshly ground pepper

1. In a casserole, heat butter and sauté mushrooms, olives and *chorizo*. Cook for about 5 to 7 minutes.

2. In a bowl blend tomato sauce and cream. Add to the mushroom mixture and simmer for 10 minutes. Season with salt and pepper. Serve over spaghetti with Parmesan cheese on the side.

5 portions

---

some good excuses to have a candlelit (not necessarily romantic) dinner

· *when the weather is nice and cool—set the table out in the porch*

· *to celebrate an anniversary—whether you are young lovers or commemorating your silver anniversary*

· *when it's someone's birthday but there's no party and no cake—just sing 'happy birthday' and blow out the candles*

· *when it's the maid's day off and you have to do the dishes—try something different to lighten and brighten the mood*

· *when there's some leftover wine from a big party the night before—take out the wine glasses*

· *when you're having fast food pizza or burgers—just for the fun of it*

· *during a brownout*

pancit bihon

Margaret Yu

$^{1}/_{2}$ kilo bihon (rice noodle)
2 cloves garlic, crushed
$^{1}/_{2}$ kilo cabbage, cut in strips
1 carrot, cut in strips
$^{1}/_{4}$ kilo small shrimps, shelled
$^{1}/_{2}$ can pork leg with mushrooms
soy sauce
salt
freshly ground pepper
1 tablespoon green onion, chopped
few drops sesame oil

1. Soften noodles in water, drain and set aside.

2. In a casserole, sauté garlic, cabbage and carrots till vegetables are cooked. Add the shrimps, then the pork leg. Stir in the noodles and mix well. If the noodles seem dry, a little water may be added. Season with soy sauce, salt and pepper. Sprinkle with the green onions and a few drops of sesame oil.

8 portions

long live the noodles

The Chinese believe that noodles must be served at a birthday party to ensure that the celebrant will have long life. Chinese restaurants have their own version of "Chinese Birthday Noodles" which is usually egg noodles topped with black mushrooms, shrimps, pork, chicken, egg strips, fried peanuts and red-colored quail eggs. The red is for good luck while the eggs symbolize birth and therefore, life.

Not wanting to take any chances, Filipinos follow this tradition and serve any kind of noodle during birthdays. The celebrant, family members and guests are urged to partake of a portion of the noodles. Filipino favorites are the pancit canton, bihon, sotanghon, Malabon or palabok. Of course, spaghetti with meat sauce is the children's favorite. Aside from the noodle dish bringing longevity and prosperity, it is a party staple because it is filling and easy to prepare.

paella de pata

Matilde Pun

1 piece beef pata *(leg)*
1 teaspoon peppercorns
1 bay leaf
¼ cup olive oil
1 small head garlic, crushed
3 large onions, chopped
2 cups California rice
1 teaspoon Spanish paprika
2 pieces chorizo Bilbao
4 cups soup stock
1 envelope saffron
1 cup garbanzos
1 red pepper, sliced
1 green pepper, sliced
2 hard-boiled eggs, sliced

1. Clean the *pata* very well. Boil once and discard the water. Boil the *pata* a second time with the peppercorns and bay leaf. Simmer till tender for about 3–4 hours. Remove *pata*, debone and cut into ½ inch cubes and set aside. Skim the fat from the stock.

2. In a *paellera* or large skillet, heat olive oil and sauté garlic and onions. Add rice and cook until it becomes opaque. Add *paprika*, *pata* and *chorizo*. Pour in the stock and sprinkle the saffron over the paella. Season with salt and pepper. Arrange the *garbanzos* and the red and green peppers on top and cook for 20 minutes. Garnish with sliced hard-boiled eggs.

5–6 portions

rice as a weather forecaster

In the provinces, some old folks believe that when the rice that they are cooking for the day is unusually steamy, this portends bad, stormy weather. The children are thus warned to play close to the house so that they can rush home for shelter when the rains begin.

bringhe

Flor Yap

1 head garlic, crushed
1 medium onion, chopped
chorizo Bilbao *lard*
1 chicken, cut in serving pieces
1 piece chorizo Bilbao, *sliced*
$^{1}/_{2}$ cup yellow ginger juice (about 2 pieces peeled
    and pounded)
1 cup malagkit rice, *washed*
1 cup rice, *washed*
4 cups thin coconut milk
1 bay leaf
patis
1 small can pimientos
2 hard-boiled eggs, quartered
banana *leaves*

1. In a large carajay, sauté garlic and onions in the lard.
Add chicken and brown, add *chorizo* and ginger juice.
Simmer for a few minutes and add the *malagkit* and the
rice. Pour in the coconut milk. Season with *patis* and
add the bay leaf. Cook covered with banana leaves.

2. When rice is cooked, pile into a serving platter and
garnish with sliced pimientos and egg.

10 portions

Ako ang nagbayo,
Ako ang nagsaing,
Saka nang maluto'y
Iba ang kumain.

– Salawikain

champorado sa gata

Bebe Marquez Cuyugan

¹/₂ kilo malagkit rice, about 2 cups
8 cups water
2 cups thin coconut milk
8 pieces native chocolates or 100 grams
    unsweetened chocolate
1 cup brown sugar
1 ¹/₂ cups thick coconut milk

1. Wash rice. Cook in a pot with the water and the thin coconut milk, stirring constantly. When cooked add chocolate and sugar and continue cooking till some of the liquid is reduced and the *champorado* is thickened. Add the thick coconut milk or serve on the side.

6 portions

Eng, eng, eng
Pot, pot, pot
Champoradong
malapot

– Filipino Nursery Rhyme

marinated kesong puti

¹/₂ cup olive oil
6 cloves garlic, sliced
2 pieces kesong puti, *sliced ¹/₂-inch thick*

1. Heat olive oil and fry garlic till golden brown. Cool.

2. Arrange the *kesong puti* in a glass dish with a cover. Pour cooled olive oil. Keep in the refrigerator for at least a day before serving.

3. Grill or fry and serve with French bread or pan de sal.

pancit lomi

Julia Teehankee

1 kilo pork bones
1/2 kilo pork liempo
   (pork belly)
1/2 kilo small shrimp
2 carrots, peeled and
   cut in strips

1/4 kilo cabbage, cut in strips
3 tablespoons soy sauce
1 kilo lomi noodles
1 bunch sibuyas Tagalog
1 bunch wansoy

1. In a large casserole put in pork bones and pork belly. Cover with about 12 cups of water and cook over a very low fire. Season with salt. When pork belly is tender, remove from casserole and slice into 1/4 × 1/2 × 1-inch strips and set aside.

2. Shell shrimps and set aside. Add the shrimp heads and shells to the soup stock and continue cooking.

3. In a separate pan, heat 2 tablespoons cooking oil. Stir fry, sliced pork, shrimps, carrots, and cabbage. Cook only until vegetables are crisp tender. Add soy sauce.

4. Peel shallots and slice thinly. Fry until lightly browned and crisp.

5. In another pot boil water and drop *lomi* noodles. Cook for about 3 minutes. Put in a colander and rinse with cold water.

6. Strain soup stock and add cooked lomi noodles. Serve soup and noodles in a bowl topped with the pork and vegetables. Sprinkle with the fried shallots and garnish with *wansoy*.

8 portions

w a n s o y

wansoy

Wansoy *are fresh coriander leaves used as topping for soups and noodle dishes or as flavoring for dipping sauces. They are sometimes called Chinese parsley because they resemble large, flat parsley leaves. Whole or chopped, they add a distinct bite to any dish.*

menu

CHINOISSERIE

Pancit Lomi

Siopao from your favorite dimsum place

Sago at gulaman

pancit malabon

Angela Villonco

¹/₂ kilo fresh pancit Malabon *noodles*
¹/₄ kilo pork, *boiled and cut into strips*
¹/₂ kilo shrimp, *cooked and shelled*
3 cups pork broth
3 tablespoons atsuete *seeds*
2 tablespoons flour
1 small head garlic, *crushed*
2 tablespoons kinchay, *chopped*
100 grams tinapa, *deboned and flaked*
100 grams chicharon, *crushed finely*
¹/₄ cup kalamansi *juice*
patis
pepper
¹/₂ kilo oysters, *cooked and shucked*
2 boiled eggs, *cut in quarters*
1 head pechay Tagalog, *blanched and sliced*

1. In a pot boil water and cook *pancit Malabon*. Drain and put aside.

2. Soak *atsuete* in pork broth, when the broth turns dark red, remove *atsuete* and blend in flour.

3. Sauté garlic and add *atsuete* mixture. Cook till thickened.

4. In a large bowl put together noodles, *atsuete* sauce, *kinchay*, *tinapa*, *chicharon*, pork, shrimps, *kalamansi* juice. Season with *patis* and pepper. Arrange attractively on a serving dish or a *bilao*. Decorate with sliced boiled eggs, oysters and *pechay*.

4–6 portions

atsuete: natural food coloring

Atsuete *seeds are tiny red seeds from annatto fruits brought to the Philippines centuries ago by the Span-iards who found the trees in Mexico. Red to orange food coloring is extracted by steeping the seeds in hot water or frying in oil. It is used to brighten some local fare such as* kare-kare, afritada, ukoy, pancit luglog *sauce and* pancit sotanghon *soup.*

a t s u w e t e

pancit luglug

Rebecca Makapugay Oliveira

1/2 *cup achuete seeds*
2 cups hot water
1 cup chicken breast, deboned, skinned and chopped
1/2 *cup fresh shrimps peeled*
1 tablespoon light olive oil
4 large garlic cloves minced
1 large onion minced
1 can cream of mushroom soup

1. Soak achuete seeds in hot water for 30 minutes. Work the achuete with your fingers to get maximum color. The water should turn red. Strain and set aside.

2. Using the steel blade of a food processor or an osterizer, puree chicken and shrimp together until smooth and fine.

3. Heat oil in a non-stick pan. Sauté garlic and onions until soft. Add chicken and shrimp puree and cook another 5 minutes.

4. Stir in the mushroom soup, breaking up the lumps and mixing thoroughly with the chicken and shrimp puree. Add achuete water slowly, stirring to keep sauce smooth. Simmer over low fire until thickened.

The recipe for this sauce is unusual but the outcome is the traditional Luglug taste but using less fat.

Toppings:

250 grams small shrimps boiled and peeled

250 grams small squid, skin removed and cut into rings and
    sautéed in olive oil and garlic

4 hard-boiled eggs, quartered

3 medium-sized tinapa, pan fried, skinned and flaked

1 cup crushed chicharon

1/2 cup toasted garlic

spring onion chopped

2 pieces bean curd cut in small cubes and fried until crisp

sliced calamansi

patis

wansoy or coriander for garnish

Assembly:

Prepare bihon noodles by bringing a pot of water to boil
with 1 tablespoon cooking oil. Put in 500 grams of
bihon, cook about 5 minutes. Drain and put in a serving
platter. Put toppings in uniform bowls and serve around
the noodles. Serve with sauce on the side.

desserts

met a woman who say the
treasure bay Grandfather

desserts

The Filipino cook is never insulted when after a full meal,
one asks for a *"pampaalis ng sawa o suya"* to cleanse the lingering
flavors left in the palate. Our food has such dominant salty,
spicy or sour flavors that leave an almost unpleasant aftertaste
in the mouth and to skip dessert would be unwise.

Filipino desserts are always sweet, sometimes too sweet.
The meal-ender can be a piece of fresh fruit in season or a ladleful
of candied fruit. Sometimes it is a custard, *gulaman* or a slice
of cake. Native *kakanin* are also eaten for dessert but because they
are usually heavy, they are more popular as merienda fare.
Whatever it is, the meal's finalé must end
on a sweet note.

cashew macaroons

Mariquita Villanueva Adriano

$^3/_4$ cup cashews, chopped finely
$^1/_2$ cup sugar
3 tablespoons flour
$^1/_3$ cup butter, melted
2 egg yolks, lightly beaten
1 tablespoon evaporated milk
2 egg whites, stiffly beaten

1. Combine cashews, sugar and flour in a bowl. Add melted butter, egg yolks and evaporated milk. Fold in egg whites. Spoon into paper lined macaroon tins, fill them up only three fourths full. Bake at 350°F till firm and golden brown

Cashew-nut
Anacardium occidentale L.

*Isang munting
prinsesa nakaupo
sa tasa*

Sagot: kasoy

97

platanillos

Pilar del Castillo

3 cups sugar
3 cups water
20 eggyolks

For filling:
1 tall can evaporated milk
¹/₃ cup sugar
¹/₃ cup cornstarch
2 tablespoons butter
1 teaspoon vanilla
6-8 marachino cherries, chopped

Fold sides to form a cone. Decorate with a cherry on the open side.

1. Combine sugar and water in a casserole and make a light syrup.

2. Beat eggyolks till light and lemon colored. Drop a tablespoon at a time in the syrup forming a circle about 3 inches in diameter. Cook till just firm. Remove and put in a tray without overlapping. Do not allow syrup to boil, remove from fire once in a while and add a little hot water when syrup gets too thick.

3. Combine filling ingredients except vanilla. Cook over medium heat till thick stirring constantly. Cool and add vanilla.

4. Lay a circle on a plate and put a tablespoon of filling in the center, fold sides to form a cone. Decorate with a cherry on the open side. Chill.

10 portions

maja blanca

Amelita Adriano Daez

4 cups thin coconut milk
2 cups buko juice
1 cup powdered milk
¹/₂ cup water
1 ¹/₄ cups sugar
¹/₂ teaspoon salt
1 cup cornstarch
1 cup water
1 can cream style corn
buko from 2 coconuts

For latik:
1 cup thick coconut milk

1. In a large casserole put all *Maja Blanca* ingredients.
Simmer over low fire for about 15 minutes. Pour into
serving dishes and cool.

2. Heat the thick coconut milk over medium heat.
When it starts to boil lower the heat and cook for about
25 minutes stirring constantly. Strain excess oil.
Sprinkle over cooled *Maja Blanca*.

Note: The addition of powdered milk might seem strange
but the result is one of the most wonderful *Maja Blancas*
I've tried.

the sower's song

by *Thomas Carlyle*

Fall gently and still,
good corn,
Lie warm in thy
earthly bed;
And stand so yellow
some morn,
For beast and man
must be fed.

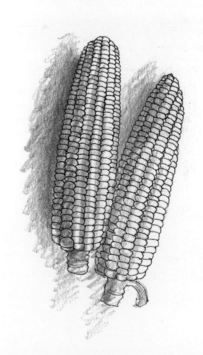

sago at gulaman

Marina Reyes Antonio

1 cup sugar
2 cups water
1 bar white gulaman, *soaked in water and drained*
3 cups cooked sago

1. Caramelize sugar and when golden brown add water and bring to a boil. Put in the softened *gulaman* and stir till completely melted. Strain into a baking pan. Cool and cut into cubes.

2. For the *sago*, make a syrup following the procedure for the *gulaman*. Continue cooking the caramelized sugar and water until syrupy. Pour boiling water over the *sago*, drain and combine with the syrup. Serve with the cubed *gulaman* with crushed ice.

6 portions

They're permanent fixtures on bus terminals, waiting sheds and supermarket exits: Sa Malamig *drinks— those large, plastic or glass jars of refreshments that come in a variety of flavors and colors. For a few pesos, one can have a glass of cold sago-gulaman, diluted canned pineapple juice (with the paper label pasted on the jar),* buko *juice with strips of* buko, *melon juice when in season, artificially-colored* kalamansi *juice with* kalamansi *halves floating on top or buko "salad," a pink concoction of* sago, gulaman, *and buko strips in a sweet, milky soup.*

Shouting "sa malamig" to attract passersby, the vendors prey on weary commuters or tired shoppers who cannot resist buying a cold drink to quench their thirst.

banana dumpling with kalamansi juice

Connie Pascal

cavendish

For pastry:
1 ¹/₂ cups flour
¹/₂ teaspoon salt
¹/₂ cup shortening or margarine
ice water

latundan

For filling:
Lacatan banana
2 tablespoons kalamansi *juice*
¹/₂ cup brown sugar
¹/₂ teaspoon cinnamon

señorita

For kalamansi *sauce:*
¹/₄ cup sugar
1 tablespoon cornstarch
1 cup kalamansi *juice*
1 tablespoon butter

1. Make the pastry by combining the flour and the salt in a bowl. With a pastry blender or two knives cut in the shortening or margarine until pea-sized pieces are formed. Sprinkle enough ice water to make the pastry stick together to form a ball. Roll out between floured wax paper sheets to form a rectangle about ¹/₄-inch thick. Cut squares of desired size.

lacatan

2. To make the filling, peel and cut the bananas about 2 inches crosswise. Sprinkle with the kalamansi juice to prevent discoloration. Combine sugar and cinnamon.

saba

3. Put a banana in the center of a pastry square, sprinkle with a teaspoon of cinnamon sugar. Moisten the edges of the pastry and pinch together all sides to seal in the banana. Brush the dumplings with milk and lightly sprinkle with cinnamon sugar. Bake at 350°F for 15 minutes till the pastry is golden brown.

4. To make the sauce, combine sugar, cornstarch and kalamansi juice in a casserole. Cook over medium heat till thick and stir in butter. Serve sauce on the side.

going bananas

Bananas are probably the most common and most readily available local fruit in the Philippines. They are easy to cultivate, require minimal care and therefore, sold relatively cheap.

The more familiar varieties include latundan *(oblong with whitish flesh), the* lacatan *(long and slender with yellowish flesh), the* señorita *(little ones sold by the baging with several clusters), the* baston *or* cavendish *variety (giant fruits exported abroad for at least $1 a piece) and the* saba *(fat, rounded and thick skinned).*

The latundan, lacatan *and* señorita *are favorite dessert or snack fruits. Overripe bananas, which have more flavor and give off a more pronounced sweet smell, are best mashed and made into banana cake or banana muffins. They can also be mixed in a batter of flour and eggs to make* maruya *or sliced thinly and fried to make crisp banana fritters.*

buko and lychee bavarian

Aurora Reyes Narciso

For first layer:
2 tablespoons Knox unflavored gelatine
3 cups buko juice

For second layer:
¹/₂ cup buko juice
2 tablespoons Knox unflavored gelatine
2 small cans thick cream
1 can condensed milk
1 can lychees, drained and quartered
2 cups buko, scraped with a spoon

1. Measure ¹/₂ cup *buko* juice and combine with the gelatine. Stand 5 minutes to soften. Heat over medium flame, stirring to melt gelatine. Add to the remaining *buko* juice and put in rectangular glass dish. Chill till firm.

2. Combine *buko* juice and gelatine and melt gelatine as in step 1. Mix with the rest of the ingredients and pour over hardened *buko* juice layer. Chill.

8 portions

bibingkang cassava

Mariquita Villanueva Adriano

3 eggs
2 cups sugar
3 cups thick coconut milk
1 cup evaporated milk
7 cups raw cassava, grated
1/4 cup butter, melted
banana leaves

For the topping:
1 cup thick coconut milk
2 tablespoons flour
1 can condensed milk
2 egg yolks
2 tablespoons grated cheese

1. Beat eggs and sugar till lemon colored. Add the rest of the ingredients. Pour into a greased 9 × 9 pan lined with banana leaves. Bake at 350°F or for 40 minutes.

2. Mix coconut milk with the flour. Add condensed milk and cook over medium heat till thick. Add eggyolks and mix well. Return to heat and cook 5 minutes more. Pour over baked *bibingka*, sprinkle with the grated cheese and broil till golden brown.

12 portions

* Refer to page 107 for cassava preparation

cassava

Locally known as kamoteng kahoy *because it looks like a branch from a tree, the cassava tuber is usually dried under the sun to eliminate the itchiness it may cause one's throat when swallowed. When cooked, the thick bark is peeled off and the starchy, fibrous, white meat is dipped in sugar and eaten. Cassava is also made into* suman, bibingka *and other native delicacies.*

leche flan

Pilar Caraballo Marquez

For caramel:
1/2 cup sugar
2 tablespoons water

For flan:
6 egg yolks
2 eggs
3/4 cup sugar
1 1/2 cups fresh milk

1. In a half gallon pan, caramelize sugar and water till golden brown. Turn caramel around pan to coat sides evenly.

2. In a bowl combine flan ingredients and mix thoroughly with a whisk or eggbeater. Strain mixture into prepared pan. Cook in a double broiler or *bano Maria* for 40 minutes until firm. Cool and keep in the refrigerator a few hours before inverting into a deep serving dish.

6–8 portions

leche flan de leche

The name Leche Flan is actually grammatically wrong because in proper Spanish, this custard of milk should be called Flan de Leche. The recipe for this favorite Filipino dessert was brought to the Philippines by the Spaniards in the 1500s. In the provinces, old folks claim that their Spanish ancestors used egg whites or albumin as cement to reinforce the structure of churches leaving bowls and bowls of egg yolks. Instead of throwing them away, these were made into delicious desserts such as the Flan de Leche and Tocino del Cielo.

mango charlotte

Virginia Roces de Guzman

¹/₂ cup sugar
1 cup water
1 tablespoon Knox unflavored gelatine
1 tablespoon water
2 egg yolks
2 tablespoons sugar
¹/₂ cup milk
2 cups mango, mashed with a fork
¹/₂ cup cream, whipped
lady fingers

1. In a casserole, put together sugar and water. Bring to boil and simmer until it thickens to a light syrup. Cool.

2. Soften gelatine in water and set aside.

3. In a casserole, combine yolks, sugar and milk. Cook over medium heat until thickened and mixture can coat a spoon. Stir in gelatine and blend until melted. Add mango puree and syrup. Cool.

4. When mixture is cool fold in whipped cream. Pour into a loaf pan lined with lady fingers. Freeze until firm. Unmold into a platter and decorate with mango balls.

10 portions

"A good dinner

sharpens the wit,

while it softens the heart."

– Doran

pichi pichi

Cely Kalaw

3 cups grated cassava
2 cups water
2 cups sugar
1 teaspoon lihiya
grated young coconut

1. Squeeze the cassava with the hands to extract the juice. In a bowl, combine the cassava, water, sugar and lihiya. Mix thoroughly and pour into small muffin tins. Steam until cassava is soft and transparent. Remove from the pan and roll in grated coconut.

how to prepare the cassava

Wash the cassava in water and brush to remove the soil. Then, slice the cassava into smaller pieces. Make a cut on the skin and peel off the bark. Choose the large roots for they are easier to peel. Remove the discolored portions which may be toxic. Grate peeled cassava and wash with water. Squeeze dry and save the pulp.

alpahol

Marina Reyes Antonio

5 pieces yellow camote
5 pieces saging na saba
3 cups water
$^1/_2$ cup water
2 cups thick coconut milk

1. Boil camote till half-cooked, drain and set aside.

2. In a casserole, caramelize sugar till deep golden brown. Add water and bring to a boil, simmer till syrupy. Add *saba* and when almost cooked, add *camote*. Continue cooking until syrup is thick and *saba* and *camote* are just tender. Serve warm or cold with the coconut milk on the side.

banana-q and company

The saba *is one banana variety which must be cooked to be enjoyed. Simply boiled till tender in a sugar syrup then served with shaved ice, it is a delicious meal-ender. In cooking, it is incorporated in some Spanish dishes such as* puchero, estofado *and* arroz a la cubana.

But the bulk of the saba *supply is eaten up by the vendors of the banana-q and the* saging na turon, *two favorite meriendas of Pinoys whether an executive secretary in Makati or a fish vendor in Divisoria.*

The name banana-q or banana-cue was copied from barbecue because to the Filipino mind, anything that is skewered onto bamboo sticks, is some kind of "cue" like kamote-cue.

buko gulaman

Marietta Adriano Roces

6 cups buko *juice*
³/4 cup sugar
2 bars white gulaman
2 tablespoons evaporated milk
1 cup buko, *scraped with a spoon*

1. In a casserole, combine *buko* juice, *gulaman* and sugar. Bring to a boil and simmer until *gulaman* is completely melted. Add the milk. Strain into a serving container and add the *buko*. Cool and refrigerate.

This recipe makes a very soft and refreshing *gulaman*. If you want a firmer consistency reduce the *buko* juice by ¹/₂ cup.

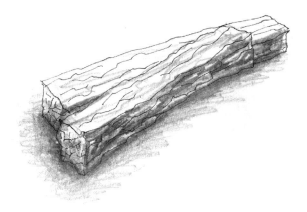

gulaman or agar-agar

Agar-agar *or* gulaman *is a natural vegetable gelatin made from seaweed. It sets without refrigeration and has a firmer texture than gelatin.* Gulaman *is sold in red, green, yellow, white and orange colored bars that make for very colorful and delicious desserts when mixed with canned or fresh fruits.*

pinipig crunch

Mariquita Villanueva Adriano

1 cup pinipig, *about 4 cups when puffed*
pinch salt
¼ cup butter
chopped casuy or peanuts
1 cup sugar
1 tablespoon water

1. In a casserole heat about 2 inches of cooking oil and fry the *pinipig*. Pour into a colander to drain off the oil.

2. Put the puffed *pinipig* in a large pan or bowl. Add salt and butter. Add nuts if you wish.

3. In a casserole put together sugar and water. Cook over medium heat till it reaches the hard ball stage. Pour over *pinipig*, tossing and turning with a wooden spoon to coat with the syrup. Form into balls and cool. Store in an airtight container.

hard ball stage

Melt sugar and water in a thick metal or non-stick pan over low to medium heat. Using a wooden spoon, stir continuously until sugar melts and begins to brown.

Test for hard ball stage by putting a drip of syrup into a glass of cold water. If it hardens like candy, it is done. If using a candy thermometer, hard-ball stage is 250°–260°F or 122°–127°C.

To melt hardened syrup, heat over double boiler. Stir until melted and use immediately.

natilla

Lily de Asis

2 cups heavy cream
1/3 cup granulated sugar
6 egg yolks
2 teaspoons vanilla
1/2 cup light brown sugar

1. In a medium-sized saucepan, heat cream over a low flame and stir in sugar gradually.

2. In a bowl, beat egg yolks with a whisk or eggbeater until thick and lemon colored. Remove cream from fire and pour half of it into the egg yolks stirring constantly, pour back into the saucepan.

3. Return saucepan to the fire and cook cream stirring all the while until mixture thickens and coats a spoon. Remove from fire and stir in vanilla.

4. Pour custard into a shallow 5-cup ovenproof dish. Set dish on a pan with about an inch of water. Bake in a preheated oven set at 325°F for 45–50 minutes until custard sets. Cool and refrigerate.

5. Set the chilled custard in a pan and surround with cracked ice. Sift the brown sugar over the custard covering the surface evenly. Broil in the oven until sugar melts. Watch carefully as sugar burns easily. Melted sugar should form a crisp golden crust. Chill custard and serve cold.

6 portions

old wives' tale about old maids

In some provinces, old folks believe that the table must not be cleared if someone at the table is still eating, especially if the one left is still unmarried. They say that this also clears away one's marriage prospects. To play safe, the table is cleared only after everyone has finished with the meal.

pandan jade

Emma Rustia Tan

2 bars green gulaman
1 ¹/₂ cups water
5 pandan *leaves*
2 cups thick coconut milk
1 ¹/₂ cups sugar

1. In a bowl soak *gulaman* bars in the water for 30 minutes.

2. In a casserole put softened *gulaman* with water, add *pandan* leaves. Boil until *gulaman* is dissolved. Discard the *pandan* leaves.

3. Reduce the heat and add the coconut milk and sugar. Stir till sugar is dissolved and mixture begins to simmer. Remove from fire and strain into a mold. When cool, refrigerate and serve cold.

new ways with pandan

Pandan *leaves or screw pine* leaves impart a special fragrance to boiled rice. A couple of these long green leaves are tucked into the sinaing *just before the rice is* cooked. Pandan *is now* being used by innovative cooks as a flavor enhancer for meat or chicken and as natural food coloring for cakes and desserts.

coconut balls

Mariquita Villanueva Adriano

3 cups buko, *grated*
1 1/2 cups white sugar
1/4 cup evaporated milk
1 strip lime peel
2 tablespoons butter
3 egg yolks

1. In a large casserole, put a *buko,* sugar, milk and lime peel. Cook over medium heat, stirring constantly until thick. Remove from fire and add butter and egg yolks. Return to fire and cook 5 minutes more.

2. Cool coconut mixture and shape into balls. Roll in sugar and wrap in cellophane.

2. Cool coconut mixture and shape into balls.

Among all the habits we Filipinos have assimilated from the Spanish, two everyday practices stand out: the siesta *and the* merienda. The siesta is the afternoon nap that must be taken to recharge one's energies. But not everyone has the time and leisure to take a siesta.

The merienda *or snack time is for everyone. Also needed to recharge one's energies with nourishment, the mid-morning* merienda *and/or the afternoon* merienda *is a must. We could say that a Filipino eats 3 1/2 or 4 meals a day, with each* merienda *equivalent to half a meal.*

There is no usual merienda *fare because we eat anything for* merienda: *a plate of* pancit, *a bowl of* champorado, *a stick of banana-cue, a sandwich, a slice of cake and coffee, a glass of halo-halo, a packet of biscuits and softdrinks.*

Merienda is so much a part of the Filipino lifestyle that the word has taken on different forms: "Mag-merienda tayo!" or "Anong merienda ngayon?" or "I'll meet you for merienda." Merienda is in our culture and part of our people—students and teachers, executives and janitors, matrons and their drivers, metro-aides and policemen: "wala ba tayong pang merienda diyan?"

guinomis

Cecile Adriano Roces

2 bars white gulaman
6 cups water
¹/₂ cup sugar

1. In a bowl put together the *gulaman* and water. Stand about 20 minutes to soften.

2. In a casserole, put in the sugar and melt over high heat. Caramelize to a deep golden brown. Add *gulaman* and water and bring to a boil and cook till the *gulaman* is all melted. Strain over a cheesecloth. Cool and cut into cubes.

For the syrup:
1 piece panocha *crushed*
1 cup water
1 cup brown sugar
thick coconut milk
toasted pinipig

1. Soak *panocha* in water a few hours or overnight till dissolved. Put in a casserole with the sugar. Bring to a boil then simmer till thick. Cool.

2. To assemble guinomis, put cubed *gulaman* in a glass with a little syrup and thick coconut milk. Add crushed or shaved ice and top with the toasted *pinipig*.

In Bulacan, a special herbal tea called "pito-pito" is known to have medicinal qualities. Made by boiling 7 leaves of 7 plants in 7 cups of water, the combination of mango, avocado, *anise,* pandan, *guava,* banaba *and* kalamata *leaves makes for an inexpensive, readily available health drink.*

jalea de mangga

Adelina Reyes Cruz

5 cups mango puree
2 1/4 cups sugar
1 1/2 tablespoons calamansi juice

1.   Mash ripe mangoes with a fork and measure out 5 cups. Combine the rest of the ingredients in a stainless steel or enamel casserole. Do not use an aluminum pan as it will react with the acid of the fruits.

2.   Bring to a boil, lower heat and simmer over low heat for an hour to an hour and fifteen minutes. The mango should be very thick and heavy to stir. Pack into clean jars. This recipe will yield about 2 cups of dense and chewy mango jam.

The original family recipe was made in such a large quantity that it took all day stirring in a giant 'kawa' over a charcoal fire. The jalea would have a mild smoky flavor.

Preserve summer

in glass jars.

Make jam.

> *—Helen Simpson*
> *20th Century*
> *English writer*

bruun butter cake

Adela Vargas Locsin

1 ³/₄ cups cake flour
2 teaspoons baking powder
³/₄ cup Bruun butter
³/₄ cup sugar
4 egg yolks
2 tablespoons milk
¹/₂ teaspoon vanilla
4 egg whites
¹/₄ cup sugar

1. Sift dry ingredients together.

2. Beat butter, add sugar gradually, beating until light and fluffy. Add egg yolks one at a time, add milk and vanilla

3. In a separate bowl, using clean beaters, beat egg whites until light with fine bubbles. Add sugar gradually until egg whites are shiny and can hold a peak. Fold into butter mixture. Pour into a large 8" × 5" loaf pan or a 9" square pan. Bake at 350°F for 30 – 35 minutes.

Bruun butter is a brand of tinned butter that has a very strong almost cheesy flavor. Regular fresh butter may be substituted but the cake will not be as rich and buttery.

cake flour

milk

eggs

116

hot pan de sal

Menchu Marcos

1 1/4 teaspoons dry yeast
1 teaspoon sugar
1 cup warm water
3 1/4 cups all purpose flour
1 teaspoon salt
1 tablespoon sugar
1 tablespoon cooking oil
1 tablespoon powdered milk
breadcrumbs

1. Combine yeast sugar and warm water. Stand 10 minutes until yeast is frothy.

2. Put the rest of the ingredients in a large bowl. Stir in yeast mixture with a wooden spoon. When dough gets too heavy to mix with the spoon, transfer dough to a lightly floured tabletop. Knead for 10 minutes until dough is smooth and elastic. Return to bowl, cover with a dishtowel and allow to rise for 1 hour.

3. Punch down the dough roll into a log about a foot long. Cut the dough into 12 pieces and roll in the breadcrumbs. Arrange in a baking tray about 2 inches apart. Allow to rise in a draft-free room for 1 hour. Pan de sals are ready to be baked when the top has bubbles showing thru. Bake in a hot oven at 375°F for 15 minutes.

index

index

index

index

index

index

Date ——————————————

Recipe ————————————————————————————————

Sourcè ————————————————————————————————

Preparation Time ——————— Cooking Time ——————— Serves ———————

Ingredients ————————————   ————————————————————

———————————————————   ————————————————————

———————————————————   ————————————————————

———————————————————   ————————————————————

———————————————————   ————————————————————

Directions ——————————————————————————————

——

——

——

——

——

——

——

——

——

——

——

——

——